93

 **St. Louis Community
College**

Forest Park
Florissant Valley
Meramec

Instructional Resources
St. Louis, Missouri

The Age of *Hair*

Recent Titles in
Contributions in Drama and Theatre Studies

THE AGE OF *HAIR*

EVOLUTION AND IMPACT OF BROADWAY'S FIRST ROCK MUSICAL

Barbara Lee Horn

Contributions in Drama and Theatre Studies,
Number 42

GREENWOOD PRESS
New York • Westport, Connecticut • London

Library of Congress Cataloging-in-Publication Data

Horn, Barbara Lee.
    The age of *Hair* / evolution and impact of Broadway's first rock
musical / Barbara Lee Horn.
       p.   cm.—(Contributions in drama and theatre studies, ISSN
0163-3821 ; no. 42)
    Includes bibliographical references and index.
    ISBN 0-313-27564-5 (alk. paper)
    1. MacDermot, Galt. *Hair.* 2. Ragni, Gerome. *Hair.* 3. Rado,
James. *Hair.* 4. Musicals—History and criticism. I. Title.
II. Series.
ML410.M117H7   1991
782.1′4166—dc20   91-15984

British Library Cataloguing in Publication Data is available.

Library of Congress Catalog Card Number: 91-15984
ISBN: 0-313-27564-5
ISSN: 0163-3821

First published in 1991

Greenwood Press, 88 Post Road West, Westport, CT 06881
An imprint of Greenwood Publishing Group, Inc.

Printed in the United States of America

The paper used in this book complies with the
Permanent Paper Standard issued by the National
Information Standards Organization (Z39.48-1984).

10 9 8 7 6 5 4 3 2 1

Copyright Acknowledgments

This book is for
my mother and father,
Lucy and Wesley Ramstein

No matter the reaction to the content, though, I suspect the form will be important to the history of the American musical. About a year ago, Ellen Stewart, LaMama herself, said she didn't care what happened to her theater group so long as she was able to effect some change on the "moribund" professional stage. Through Mr. O'Horgan, Miss Stewart has got her revolution, significant in its way as "Pal Joey," "Oklahoma!" and "West Side Story."

John J. O'Connor
The Wall Street Journal
May 1, 1968

Contents

Acknowledgments

Although the title page bears my name only, I consider this study to be a collaborative endeavor. Without the generous assistance and endless patience of the people listed here, this book could never have been written. And while each of them has provided me with invaluable help, I must single out *Hair*'s authors, Gerome Ragni, and most especially James Rado, for special thanks. In alphabetical order, the other members of *Hair*'s family and friends who have furnished me with their unique insights are: Clive Barnes, Isabelle Blau, Joseph Campbell Butler, Michael Butler, Bertrand Castelli, Lorrie Davis, Jules Fisher, Gerald Freedman, Martin Gottfried, Galt MacDermot, Melba Moore, Tom O'Horgan, Ellen Stewart, and Robin Wagner. I am grateful to Professor Albert Bermel of Lehman College for the encouragement and direction that I needed to complete the text. Thanks to Dr. Bill DiFazio of St. John's University for his comments on the sixties. I deeply appreciate Dr. Donna Geffner of St. John's University for her constant and much-needed support. And, again, my thanks to my own flower children, Willard, Lara, Robert, and Richard, who have patiently endured my academic pursuits with me.

Introduction

The Broadway musical, while recognized as a distinct and uniquely American art form, does not occupy a central position in theater arts scholarship. Despite its widespread popularity—indeed, partially owing to its mass appeal—it has seldom received serious attention from the academic community. Instead, it has generally been treated as a marginal, even trivial, artifact or pastime. Although there is a growing body of well-written, fully-documented studies devoted to either the genre as a whole or, more rarely, to individual shows, most books about the Broadway musical are either bald descriptive chronicles or decorative coffee table books. The intellectual's tendency to relegate analyses of Broadway musicals to the lower corner of the theater arts page assumes additional force when an author's scope is confined to a single production. With respect to the study of the 1960s rock musical *Hair*, bias lends additional momentum to this predisposition. Why would any student of the theater devote the requisite time and energy to prepare a full-length treatment on a show as inherently "insignificant" as *Hair*?

Adopting the plausible premise that an art form's popularity does not automatically consign it to scholarly obscurity, an answer to this question begins with the recognition that *Hair* was a milestone in the history of the Broadway theater.

It was the first rock musical on Broadway. Theatrically innovative, if not unique, it reflected the lifestyle of the hippies.
One of the most successful musicals in the history of Broadway, *Hair* ran for five years and a record 1,750 performances
at the Biltmore, and thousands upon thousands of showings
outside of New York. While other musicals have eclipsed its
run, *Hair* spread farther and faster than any other musical in
the history of Broadway. Fourteen national companies ran
concurrently with *Hair*'s Broadway run, as did a score of international companies. Eleven cast albums were recorded,
most representative of the foreign productions. *Forbes* magazine reported that during its first two years alone, some 4
million people saw *Hair* and the show grossed $22,300,000.[1]
Between its Biltmore opening and the present, *Hair* has
grossed over $80 million from its American productions, and
perhaps an equal or larger amount from those staged interna-
tionally.[2] Without stars and extravagant sets, the musical was
capitalized for $150,000, the 10 percent overcall was never
exercised, and the limited partners were paid a thousand-to-
one on their minimal $10,000 investments.[3] Producer Michael
Butler made a lot of people millionaires and was "delighted
to do so."[4]

As a revelation of the hippie lifestyle, the production
shared in the universal appeal of an international movement.
Thus, the most compelling reason for looking back at *Hair* is
not specific to musical theatre but to its historical and cultural context—to the late sixties and the "Age of Aquarius."
As Clive Barnes asserted, "*Hair* summed it up better than
any other piece of American theater."[5] *Hair* was undeniably
the *zeitgeist* of the times. A synthesis of despair and hope,
Hair marshaled an uncompromising assault against the social
evils of the day and held forth a vision of a humanistic epoch
yet to come.

Successful, innovative, and socially relevant, with superla-
tives attached to each of these dimensions, the question
remains: Why turn to *Hair* at this late date? The answer is

that a full generation later *Hair* and the moment in time that it captured so accurately have begun to exercise a magnetic, almost mystical, pull upon those who lived through the 1960s and those born thereafter. For many adult Americans, no period in their lifetime evokes more vivid memories than the 1960s. Mention the sixties today among members of the baby boom generation and you will invariably elicit an emotionally charged response. Part of the current fascination can be ascribed to a nostalgia that attends the remembrance of things past intensified by generational bonds forged in the crucible of turbulent experience. But there is more at work than mere nostalgia. For better or for worse, the 1960s left an indelible imprint upon the American psyche, one that continues to find expression in manifold domains and unexpected ways. In virtually every artistic medium, from fiction to television, the 1960s have staged a remarkable comeback. (As I am revising this introduction, Public Television is airing a six-hour series over three nights called *Making Sense of the Sixties*.) Nor has academia been immune from this resurgence of interest in the sixties. When the University of California added a course on ''Religion and the Impact of the Vietnam War'' to its curriculum, it was so over-subscribed that the lecture class had to be videotaped to accommodate the enrollment.[6] Since most of those in attendance were in their late teens or early twenties, nostalgia alone does not explain the overwhelming popularity of the lecture series. Not coincidentally, after a twentieth anniversary reunion concert performance by *Hair*'s original cast members, staged at the United Nations in May 1988, literally dozens of *Hair* revival productions have been mounted throughout the United States.

For now, we will leave aside the question of why this is taking place, offering some speculative interpretation about the resurgence of interest in *Hair* and the sixties at this study's conclusion, hoping that the reader will come to his or her own opinion while moving through the text. What seems plain, even at this point, is that the sixties have something personal to say about our lives today, what they have become, and what they might still become. That being the case, *Hair* is one central channel through which this message is being conveyed.

Very little of substance has been written about *Hair*. The only book-length work dedicated exclusively to the show is *Letting Down My Hair* by former Biltmore tribe member Lorrie Davis,[7] and it consists primarily of insider anecdotes. Owing to the paucity of published research materials, the bulk of this study rests upon two sets of interviews conducted by the author with individuals who either had a direct hand in *Hair*'s creation or some uniquely valuable insight into the musical. The first round of talks took place between October 1977 and March 1982, while the author was gathering material for her doctoral dissertation. These discussions included interviews with both of *Hair*'s New York directors, Gerald Freedman (Public Theater) and Tom O'Horgan (Biltmore Theatre); with Galt MacDermot (composer of *Hair*'s score); and with Robin Wagner and Jules Fisher, the scenic designer and lighting director, respectively, for the Biltmore production. A far more extensive and intensive set of interviews was completed for the present book in the first half of 1990. In addition to re-interviews with Freedman, O'Horgan, and MacDermot, this search included invaluable sessions with *Hair*'s authors, Gerome Ragni and James Rado, as well as Biltmore producer Michael Butler, executive producer Bertrand Castelli, international production coordinator Isabelle Blau, and Biltmore cast members Joseph Campbell Butler, Melba Moore, and Lorrie Davis. Lastly, New York theater critics Clive Barnes and Martin Gottfried offered their insightful comments, as did Ellen Stewart (founder of the LaMaMa Experimental Theatre Club). Each of these people is mentioned in the acknowledgments preceding this introduction. At risk of redundancy, I must say that without their patient and generous assistance this book would not have been possible.

NOTES

1. Cited in Abe Laufe, *Broadway's Greatest Musicals* (New York: Funk & Wagnalls, 1969), 362.

2. Interview with James Rado, New York City, March 25, 1990.

3. Rado interview.

4. Interview with Michael Butler, New York City, April 3, 1990.

5. Interview with Clive Barnes, New York City, April 19, 1990.

6. "In Popular Class, Lessons Concern the Vietnam War," *The New York Times*, April 22, 1990, 43-44.

7. Lorrie Davis and Rachel Gallagher, *Letting Down My Hair* (New York: Arthur Fields, 1973).

The Age of *Hair*

Chapter 1

Hair and the Hippies

Hair is many things. Thematically, it is an antiestablishment protest vehicle that took dramatic and satiric aim at war, racism, sexual repression, and other societal evils. Theatrically, the show is a milestone in the evolution of the Broadway musical. But above all, *Hair* is a reflection of the hippies and the sixties. Beginning in 1965, co-authors Gerome Ragni and James Rado gathered material for *Hair*, observing, inquiring, and in a sense becoming one with the hippies of New York City's Greenwich Village. The field notes and creative jottings that came out of their investigations served as *Hair*'s basic stuff. A combined interest in the theatrical experience and the social concerns of the day resulted in a show that gave expression to hippie values, voice to hippie feelings, and stage life to hippie activities. Thus, to fully understand the meaning of *Hair*, let us first turn to the hippies themselves.

ORIGINS

The term *hippie* was coined by newspaper columnist Michael Fallon in an article in the September 5, 1965, edition of the *San Francisco Examiner*.[1] Fallon noted that local tourist buses had added the Haight-Ashbury district to their

rounds, enabling sightseers to get a glimpse of the neighborhood's "weirdo" residents. Initially, the term was synonymous with "beatnik." Not long after Fallon's article, teams
of researchers were sent out into the field—the Haight, the
East Village in New York, and various other hippie enclaves
that were amassing—to describe the second generation of
beats. Their studies established the hippies as both a subculture and a counterculture: a subset of the parent culture
which radically opposed many of society's norms. Significant
diversity within the hippie counterculture was noted: "drug
groups, nudist groups, vegetarians, communes, Jesus freaks,
Krishna devotees, and virtually hundreds of other subdivi-
sions of the larger group called hippies."[2] Some were involved in the drug scene while others were simply mystics;
there were those who were "simply living" as well as self-
seekers, the Diggers, and the Hell's Angels.[3] Mike Brake concluded that the term *hippie* covered a vast array of bohemian
and student subcultures, and as with the beats there was a
hard core of artistic-literary intelligentsia with an aristocracy
of rock musicians and a vast following of lifestyle rebels.[4]

In attempting to enumerate the salient characteristics of a
hippie, Kenneth Keniston analyzed the style of the "post-
modern youth" and identified five outstanding features:
fluidity, flux, change, and movement, both ideational and
spatial; exclusive identification with members of their own
generation; emphasis upon personalism and participation;
ambivalence toward technology; and adherence to the prin-
ciple of nonviolence.[5] William Partridge described the distin-
guishing features of the hippie as isolation from the larger
American society; experimentation with alternatives to life in
the larger society; intimacy in social relations; communal
intoxication; dependence upon esoteric views of the world;
and transience or mobility.[6] Brake observed the major characteristics as passive resistance; movement; disassociation, ex-
pressivity, subjectivity; and individualism.[7]

While a conclusive definition was elusive, social scientists agreed that many of the hippies had become alienated from their economically, educationally, and socially privileged families. They came from affluent upper-middle class, politically liberal, secular families, had excellent educations, and attended prestigious colleges. In many cases, the youth were the brightest students. They were extremely articulate. And when they dropped out, society was at a loss to explain why.

The reasons for the emergence of the hippie counterculture were numerous and varied. As a manifestation of generational conflict, the movement was not unique. Throughout history youth has been viewed as being in conflict with the older generation. Adolescent rebellion, psychologists tell us, is inherent in becoming an adult. In the case of the hippies, the concern with developing a personal position vis-à-vis society at large may be viewed as an exaggerated avatar of adolescent angst.

Discontent with Western civilization can be seen as another factor leading to the hippie counterculture. Commenting on the repressive and inhibiting nature of contemporary Western civilization, R. D. Laing notes, "Freud insisted that our civilization is a repressive one. There is a conflict between our demands for conformity and the demand of our instinctive energies, explictly sexual. Freud could see no resolution to this antagonism, and he came to believe that in our time the possibility of simple natural love between human beings had already been abolished."[8] The thesis of a repressive society inhibiting sexual energies in order to harness the psychic power necessary to perform the work of the world has been advanced in a variety of ways. They all lead to the possible conclusion that the hippie movement was an attempt to overcome modern civilization's inhibitions by a new and intense preoccupation with libidinous expression and subsequent release.

Still another set of factors which social analysts see as critical to the emergence of the hippie counterculture resides in the emotional configuration of the modern nuclear family.

Many critics blamed the movement on middle-class parents who were overly permissive, gratifying their children's every whim in a manner that was unprecedented. Roszak commented that the hippies were "spoiled kids" in an arrested state of development, occupying a limbo stage "between a permissive childhood and an obnoxiously conformist world."[9]

The parents of the baby-boomers had grown up during the Great Depression, and they had known the destruction of World War II. But the Depression was over as were the deprivations of the war, and a sense of well-being prevailed. As the economy flourished, Americans acquired consumer goods at an unparalleled rate, joining the ranks of the affluent. This was the silent generation of the fifties—conservative and conformist. Highly valued was material betterment and the hard work necessary to attain it. Any upsets, social or economic, were to be avoided.

The prosperity of the fifties translated into the baby boom, the housing boom, and the college student boom. Parents moved to the suburbs for their kids, lived their lives for their kids, and catered to their kids' every desire. Yet, while the hippies grew up knowing how good material comfort would be, they recognized the hypocrisy in their lives. While cornucopia and conformity were supposed to buy contentment, satisfaction seemed decidedly amiss. Revealing their own insecurities, parents constantly recounted "when-I-was-your-age" Depression stories. They harped upon the need for sexual responsibility and mental clarity while engaging in extramarital escapades and battles with the bottle. Trapped in her perfect house, a well-upholstered consumer paradise, mother's talents and emotions found little expression within her marriage. And caught on his own treadmill to pay the bills, father's idealism and youthful dreams were crushed by the realities of adult life. Mothers openly disparaged husbands, who became weak and inadequate models to be overthrown, as is the case with small adolescent boys, for the exclusivity of mother's love. In this case, the "boys" carried the rebellion to the destruction of male authority in general.[10]

Hippies dropped out, asserting that although they had been offered every material advantage and opportunity, they had experienced a painful lack of love and genuine emotional interaction in the family. As this theory postulates, if parents had given them more love, there would not have been the sex, the drugs, the love-ins, the attempts at a kind of "universal love" that they had been unable to learn as individuals.[11]

Another theoretical cause of the movement may be found in the lack of participation by young people in the outside or "real" world. Afforded an extended education apart from the vocational grind, they had not experienced participation in the mainstream of social activity. Thus, the key word in the youth's collective attitude was *participation*, which became a strong motivational force. Without participating in society, the youths were unable to develop their own value system. Confronted by this lack and the driving need to see themselves as individuals, they simply inverted the values of their parents.

As a counterculture, hippies appeared to identify society's prevalent and important values, and then consciously to replace them with antithetical values. For example, if holding a job was considered socially desirable, then being unemployed became a requisite for membership in the group. Anyone who ranked work higher than "freedom" clearly exhibited mental lacunae.

The notion of freedom equated to instant gratification, and conventional work clearly did not fulfill this requirement. Following this line of hippie wisdom, "doing your own thing" became synonymous with avoiding conventional work, a dedication to self-discovery, and concern with personal needs and gratification. The hippies were the leisured youth with time and money to spend. They dropped out of society, but society did not drop them: "But luckily for him, society sticks around, because the hippie is a parasite. The straight world supports him. Without this country's prosperity, there could be no hippies. They'd have nobody to bum from, nobody to give them easy jobs to tide them over the winter. There would be no leisure time in which to practice being hip."[12]

During the 1960s, economic prosperity caused the rapid growth of higher education. Parents placed a high priority on college education, which they believed was the route upward to the land of plenty. In cloistered classrooms, students were exposed to contradictory messages regarding C. P. Snow's two cultures. From professors in the natural sciences, they gleaned the importance of scientific objectivity and goal-oriented principles. From the liberal arts and social sciences, they received a subjective, ideal-oriented perspective, that emphasized ethical relativism and the quest for self-knowledge. Failing to integrate the two, many of the youths allied themselves with their softer-discipline mentors, only to realize later that liberal arts did not accord with the demands of the real world and getting a job. Merit, as opposed to ascriptive characteristics, no longer proved the sole criterion of occupational status and advancement. While these students had demonstrated their talents in the university and looked forward to prestigious positions upon graduation, such was not the case. The economy had become less labor-intensive, the number of elite jobs reduced to a minimum. Faced with the alternative of accepting less than high-level employment, many of the students just dropped out.[13]

With the escalation of American miltary involvement in Southeast Asia in 1965 and the restoration of the draft, the armed forces became the "employer" willing to absorb the youth. Overnight young people developed a sense of immediacy in opposing U.S. imperialism, as they came to recognize what "ugly American" meant. In the opinion of leftist political analysts, the hippie movement was a protest against worldwide American imperialism, a struggle in the "belly of the beast."[14] Although most of the hippies were comparatively apolitical, some did pay lip service to the barbs of the New Left against American policies at home and abroad. Threatened by the very real risk of being drafted, many of the young men and women began to participate in antiwar protests, from mass marches in Washington, D.C., to not registering for the draft. Above all else, the Vietnam debacle crystallized the youth's opposition to their government and to the American war machine.

Prior deviant subcultures provided a legacy to the hippies. The bohemian existential movement had spread from Paris throughout Europe and North America after World War II. Two decades later, a portion of this bohemian subculture could be seen in the hippie movement, as relayed to American youth by the Beat Generation of the 1950s. Most importantly, the civil rights struggle of the 1950s and 1960s served as a model for organized protest. Although the hippies don't appear to have immediate precursors, the bohemians, the beats, and the freedom riders provided them with anticonformist and antiestablishment role models.

The impersonal nature of the technological age also encouraged 1960s youth to drop out. The parent culture was a generation enamored of science with an inexhaustible faith in the capacity of reason, but their grip on reality proved only to depersonalize and destroy. People were being reduced to automatons, and the menacing threat of nuclear warfare and mass annihilation, which weighed heavily on young psyches, contributed immensely to a live-for-the-moment mentality.

In the final analysis, the sixties were a decade of protest and turmoil, the tone set by a generation of restless and rebellious students with progressive educations from prestigious universities, who were very much aware of the evils in society—the war in Vietnam, racial injustice, poverty, environmental despoliation, technological dehumanization, and bizarre political assassinations. Simply stated, says sociology professor Bill DiFazio, the counterculture was a reaction to all forms of authority: the family first, the school, the busi-

ness, the state, and the war machine. The young generation
was expected to conform to those five forms of authority as
had their parents, but the sixties were about alternatives and a
way of saying: "No, I'm not going to be a part of these
authority structures. I'm concerned with myself, and with my
body, and I'm really going to develop a body politic. And a
body politic was what truly came out of their bodies, and
their thinking about their place in the world, and how they
wanted to be in the world. And they didn't want to be in a
world which was already decided for them."[15]

The civil rights movement contributed most to the counterculture, the beats decidedly less so. As DiFazio sees it, the
beats who came into the group, like Allen Ginsberg, Tuli
Kupferberg, and Ken Kesey, were transformed. The beats
were cynics, and they were never politicized.[16] The sixties
were about possibility and potentiality, and they were a time
of significant social movement. They were about the rejection
of different forms of institutional authority, and more importantly, they were about the creation of new possibilities.
Some of the possibilties were not viable, although many of
them were: the ecological movement, the feminist movement,
the sexual revolution, the black movement, the peace movement, and the movement to rekindle a more participatory,
more active democracy.[17] The experts were the "avatars of
power," but none of the experts had the answers. And the
sixties were about, "Hey, Hey, LBJ, how many kids did you
kill today? They were about the creation of new possibilities.
The young were no longer going to accept power from above
as being correct. And you didn't need to be a weatherman to
tell which way the wind was blowing."[18]

FORMS OF EXPRESSION

The hippie world view was externalized by various means
of expression involving appearance, behavior, and communi-

cation. The Beatles and other British rock groups introduced the trend, and "longer hair and other flamboyant affectations" became the fashion of the day. Hair was their flag. The antiestablishment cranial adornment rejected the corporate appearance, gave expression to one's sense of individuality and naturalism, and provided a sense of status within the ranks. Females also chose freer and longer styles, abandoning conformist fifties bouffants and tight perms. For both genders, long hair stood for an advanced approach to unisex lifestyle, very much confusing gender distinction. The typical establishment response was, "Is that a he or a she?"

Hippie fashion statements were of two basic modes: antimaterialistic or flamboyant. Drab work clothes, dungaree shirts, and pea coats served as a rejection of materialism. Ornamental outfits, featuring apparel from other lands and other times, were also highly visible. Unique costumes bedecked with beads, feathers, jewelry, and body paintings were signs of individual freedom, which countered the parent culture's regimentation. Garments produced in Third World countries, those made to resemble the popular Nehru shirt, natural cottons, and denims, were a reaction against mass-produced synthetic goods. Some of the dress can be seen as a nostalgic yearning for the past, as hippies literally "put on history." Males wore military uniforms from World War II or the Civil War and the traditional garb of the American Indians, and females cultivated the "granny look" with long, flowing turn-of-the-century dresses and wire-rimmed "granny glasses."

While the typical hippie gathering featured an eclectic assortment of laid-back styles, it might include the preferred dress of nothing at all. Consistent with themes of freedom and naturalism, the naked body was an esthetic object to be glorified and adored.

As a subculture or counterculture, the youth developed their own jargon, "rapping" in a ritualized form of communication. During rap sessions, frequently accompanied by marijuana use, hippies freely "shared" their thoughts about drugs, the draft, society's evils, mystical philosophies, and other avenues to self-knowledge. Lofty rhetoric and narrative coherence were replaced by disturbing vacancies in conversations, inarticulate expressions like "wow," "far out," and "hassle" that were used in any number of contexts, and obscenities which served not so much to demean the parent language as to express outrage.

Psychedelic drugs, like marijuana, peyote, and LSD, and other mind-altering substances were a part of the communal setting, taken not for fun and games but for the attainment of higher levels of consciousness. These hallucinogens were seen as liberating agents, allowing their users to clear away the cobwebs of the mind and lead them into the substratum of reality hidden beyond the physical world. Nor were the substances chemically addictive. Hippies distinguished between positive and negative drugs, rejecting alcohol, nicotine, tranquilizers, and other additive narcotics, such as heroin. According to their perceptions, hallucinogens raised consciousness levels, while narcotics and alcohol blurred the mind, distorted reality, and were used only as agents of escapism.

Finally, rock was the music of the hippies. It was to rock music that the inarticulate group turned as a mode of expression. Unlike reading or the traditional visual arts, music was an activity that could easily be shared. Stemming from minority and Third World origins, rock music provoked the establishment with its aggressive, deafening sound, pulsating rhythms, and associated drug use. Undeniably, the vast majority of performers and audience at any hippie rock performance were "high" or under the influence of some type of hallucinogenic drug, the effects of which served to unite the group in a communal celebration of shared values and beliefs which deliberately undercut the straight world.

Rock swept the country with the arrival of the Beatles in 1964. Through the 1967 release of *Sgt. Pepper's Lonely*

Hearts Club Band, unindoctrinated youth were exposed to hippie lifestyles as proclaimed in the songs of the Beatles. Perceiving *Sgt. Pepper* as a milestone in the evolution of Western music, the youth dismissed all other forms of music as antiquated and turned to rock—the music that joined together the youthful tribes of love.

Theater is a reflection of the society that produces it, and in this case, *Hair* is a reflection of the hippies. Having discussed the hippies, let us turn to the theatrical context from which *Hair* originated: the avant-garde off-off-Broadway theater of the 1960s.

NOTES

1. Bruce Cook, *The Beat Generation* (New York: Charles Scribner, 1971), 200.

2. William L. Partridge, *The Hippie Ghetto: The Natural History of a Subculture* (New York: Holt, Rinehart and Winston, 1973), 10.

3. Sherri Cavan, *Hippies of the Haight* (St. Louis: New Critics Press, 1972), 28.

4. Mike Brake, *The Sociology of Youth Culture and Youth Subcultures* (London: Routledge & Kegan Paul, 1980), 93.

5. Kenneth Kenniston, *Young Radicals: Notes on Committed Youth* (New York: Harcourt Brace Jovanovich, 1968), 275-285.

6. Partridge, 64-67.

7. Brake, 101-103.

8. R. D. Laing, *The Divided Self: An Existential Study in Sanity and Madness* (Harmondsworth, England: Penguin Books, 1960), 11-12.

9. Theodore Roszak, *The Making of a Counter Culture* (Garden City, N.Y.: Doubleday, 1968), 35.

10. Kenniston, 337.

11. D. L. Earisman, *Hippies in Our Midst* (Philadelphia: Fortress Press, 1968), 17.

12. Cecilia Holland, "I Don't Trust Anybody under 30," *Saturday Evening Post* (August 10, 1968): 11.

13. Roszak, 30.

14. Jean François Revel, *Without Marx or Jesus: The New American Revolution Has Begun* (New York: Dell Press, 1970), 209.

15. Interview with William DiFazio, Department of Sociology and Anthropology, St. John's University, Jamaica, N.Y., November 5, 1990.

16. DiFazio interview.

17. DiFazio interview.

18. DiFazio interview.

Chapter 2

Experimental Roots

By the time that *Hair* arrived on Broadway in April 1968, the musical comedy genre had become formulaic. Critics like Walter Kerr and Tom Prideaux lamented that "the novelty of *Oklahoma!* had worn off, and that new ideas and 'gimmicks' are needed. Kerr even recommended subordinating the plot again to the music and dance, noting that the musical comedy books are seldom more than 'drama at half-mast.' "[1]

The book musical had reigned supreme until *Fiddler on the Roof* (1964) which signaled to many the end of the golden age of the American musical. The seeds for a new type of musical theater were already in the experimental stage. *West Side Story* (1957), while not recognized at the time (*The Music Man*, won the Tony that year), "would not only become the first outright dance musical but the progenitor of the concept musical."[2] Choreographer-director Jerome Robbins had conceived the show in terms of transposing Shakespeare's tragic *Romeo and Juliet* into a modern New York City setting. With this unifying production idea, the show's book moved to the background and greater emphasis was placed on the score and dance movements.[3] *Fiddler on the Roof*, Robbins's next creation, continued the innovative trend of submerging dialogue and extending the emphasis on musical and dance sequences with a production idea based on the portrayal of the *shtetl* on stage.[4]

Following these two musicals, Robbins retired from Broadway to his American Theatre Laboratory, a studio founded to continue the experimentation he had begun, and finally to the New York City Ballet where he would ultimately become artistic director. No longer a part of the theater scene, the choreographer-director's legacy passed to Harold Prince who had produced the two shows *West Side Story* and *Fiddler on the Roof*. Prince refined his mentor's trailblazing genius in his own direction of the 1966 production of *Cabaret*, the "concept" for which was staging the performances of the Kit Kat Klub of Berlin. Scenes in the cabaret did not further plot or build character, but actualized the concept of decadence. While *Cabaret* was still not a fully realized concept musical (it was half conventional integrated book musical, half production-oriented), it was "Harold Prince [who] created the musical theater's first production-oriented scripts—the script for concept musicals, correlating text with performance."[5] Allowing for the production to develop from the performance idea, Prince's *Company* (1970) is considered a milestone in its plotless look at Manhattan's East Side marriages, continuous music, and emphasis on production techniques— the first fully realized concept musical.

The seventies were most notable for the concept musical. Experimentation was beginning in the hands of Hal Prince, but at the time that *Hair* appeared on Broadway in April 1968, musicals for the most part were not very innovative.

OFF-OFF BROADWAY:
THE EXPERIMENTAL THEATER

Prior to the 1960s, most of the off-Broadway musicals (*The Fantasticks* was an exception) had become as unimaginative in form and content as had their Broadway counterparts. While the integrated musical might almost be regarded as a conservative form in its resistance to change, this conservatism was contrary to the dramatic theater of the same period. During the 1950s and 1960s, the avant-garde or experimental theater proliferated with the seminal presentation of Beckett's *Waiting for Godot* in 1953. The play embodied the helplessness and bewilderment of modern man, and helped to popularize the work of many contemporary playwrights, including Genet, Ionesco, Pinter, Stoppard, and Albee, as well as the efforts of experimental directors like Peter Brook and Jerzy Grotowski. Beckett's work was preceded by the Dadaist and Surrealist movements in theater, and the prophetic visions of Antonin Artaud's "theater of cruelty," designed to strip away the layers of civilization—to liberate the repressed unconscious—to force people to see themselves as they are.

Polish director Grotowski was the foremost figure in experimental theater when *Hair* made its first appearance. An advocate of the "poor theatre," Grotowski rejected the elaborate trappings of conventional drama. While he sometimes employed innovative sets, his stagings focused upon the actors. Script, scenery, costumes, makeup, lighting effects, and even the stage platform were reduced to a minimum. Group creation during rehearsal played a significant part in actual performances. While *Hair* was shifting from the downtown Public Theater to Broadway, Grotowski and his New York City Performance Group were staging performances with all the experimental techniques, which included an interest in ritual and ceremony, textual rearrangement, improvisation, and expressive gymnastics.

During the 1960s, the New York theater continued to be revitalized by off-Broadway groups. The most influential was the Becks' The Living Theatre, a repertory company begun in 1946 with an interest in poetic drama and nonrealistic production techniques. After staging Gelber's *The Connection* in 1959, which blurred the line between art and life, the group's attention veered to improvisation and collectively created stage productions, and to the ritual, the nonverbal, the assault, and other Artaudian theater of cruelty manifestations. When the Becks' theater was closed in 1963 for failure to pay taxes, the company migrated to Europe, where its crusade against esthetic and sociopolitical restraints became more aggressively radical. (They returned to the United States in 1968).[6]

As financial concerns became the Becks' nemesis, they became the nemesis of off-Broadway in general. Broadway's commercialism and Actor's Equity caught up with the off-Broadway scene, compelling adventuresome artists and producers to look elsewhere for alternate budget-cutting theater spaces. They found them in Soho, Greenwich Village, and the Bowery. In 1958, Joe Cino turned his Caffe Cino into an arts center, and by 1961, his coffeehouse doubled as a home for the productions of aspiring playwrights. As his influence spread, nonprofit amateur productions in which enthusiasm replaced professionalism appeared in other unconventional theater spaces—in lofts, garages, studios, and even churches—and off-Broadway experimentation passed to off-off-Broadway. In that same year, 1961, Ellen Stewart, the most influential of all the off-off-Broadway producers, would tinkle her small handbell, announcing LaMama's theatrical debut. LaMama and the LaMaMa Experimental Theatre Club, which was organized as a private club to circumvent laws governing public performances, would eventually find a permanent home for the young playwrights Stewart nurtured. LaMama went on to worldwide renown, generating an international network of experimental clubs. But in its infancy, productions were held in a succession of East Village basements and walk-ups. Audiences were asked to make contributions of one dollar, revenues were meager, and rarely was anybody paid. Yet, what nonprofit LaMaMa lacked in cash it made up in talent. Stewart's growing reputation as a producer who encouraged budding young talent enabled her to

attract a circle of young unconventional playwrights, directors, and actors. Among her cadre was director Tom O'Horgan (*Hair*'s Broadway director) who lead the LaMaMa ETC
company, and actor Gerome Ragni via affiliations with the
Open Theatre, which she hosted at her theatrical space.

In 1963, several talented actors (including Ragni) who had
studied with Nola Chilton found themselves in search of a
mentor when Chilton emigrated to Israel.[7] Representatives of
the group asked Joseph Chaikin, a member of the Living
Theatre as well as a member of the Chilton group, to assume
leadership. Chaikin agreed, but made it clear that he didn't
want to be just a teacher. He wanted to leave the Living
Theatre, and, like Brook and Grotowski, form his own company. The result was a workshop ensemble called the Open
Theatre, described by Gottfried as a "shoestring group of
enthusiastic directors, writers, and actors who were justifi-
ably disgusted with the idiotic standards of mainstream New
York theatre."[8] Chaikin had been a member of the Living
Theatre since 1959. He had appeared in the plays of Piran-
dello, Brecht, and Gelber, and from experience he knew the
demands of nonnaturalistic performance. His directorial
approach combined aspects of Grotowski with the Living
Theatre's sociopolitical concerns, but without direct participation of the audience. Following Artaud's theories, "new
myths" were explored and created during the workshop set-
tings, and improvisation was used freely during performance.
Fundamental to Chaikin's work was an interest in transfor-
mational reality and the games and role-playing theories of
human behavior structured as a basis for theater training by
Viola Spolin and Paul Sills. Like Grotowski, Chaikin was interested in experimentation, and not in the demands of commercial or immediate production. He had attempted workshops unsuccessfully with the Living Theatre troupe. But
with the ex-Chilton group, he would have his laboratory to
explore nonpsychological characters and nonnaturalistic
material, as demanded by the new experimental plays.

Several of the directors, writers, and actors within the Open Theatre company had already worked at Cafe La-Mama, as they had at other off-off-Broadway theaters, when in the 1965-66 season Stewart arranged for the Open Theatre troupe to appear at her theater one week a month. While the opportunity was welcomed by the company, it divided group loyalties, and the company became more a nominal umbrella for individual scripted plays rather than a workshop of orignal intent. On May 21, 1966—Armed Forces Day—the Open Theatre presented one of its most provocative productions, Megan Terry's *Viet Rock*.[9] This was the first full-length play that had been developed improvisationally by playwright and ensemble during Saturday workshops. During these workshops, actors had examined the Vietnam War: "They discussed, abstracted and improvised newspaper clippings, television accounts, and first-hand observation of events in both the United States and Vietnam. The motives behind the violence were examined; patriotic rhetoric was taken apart; the feelings aroused by the events of the war were questioned. Gradually a pastiche of patriotic skits, scenes of warfare, and dramatic comments emerged."[10]

Viet Rock became the story of young American men inducted, trained, and sent to Vietnam to fight, to kill, and to be killed. An anti-Vietnam War theme served as a loose framework for a series of transformation scenes depicting war and destruction. The subtitle "a folk war movie" implied a cinematic structure, one scene dissolving into the next. *Viet Rock* ends with the bomb exploding, mass annihilation, bodies in a heap. A chorus of the dead chants, "Who needs war." After a brief silence, the actors rise one by one in slow motion as fragile angels, and go to mingle with the audience to "communicate the wonder and the gift of being alive."[11]

Gottfried describes Terry's plays at LaMama as "musicals without music. There was so much movement in them. They were really choreographed, and done from the point of view of theater rather than drama."[12] There were many parallels to *Hair*—the anti-Vietnam War theme, the structure, the directorial approach, the collective creativity of the group. Although the piece was not a musical, it included six rock songs and an acoustical guitar. And most importantly, just as Terry scripted *Viet Rock* from the collective creativity that emerged from the Open Theatre workshop techniques and discovery period, Ragni and Rado would rewrite much of the Broadway *Hair* from the collaborative ensemble creativity that developed under O'Horgan's leadership during the rehearsal-workshop period.

NOTES

1. Glenn Loney, "Musical Comedy," in *The Reader's Encyclopedia of World Drama*, John Gassner and Edward Quinn, eds. (New York: Thomas Y. Crowell, 1969), 596.

2. Martin Gottfried, *Broadway Musicals* (New York: Harry N. Abrams, 1979), 103.

3. Loney, 592.

4. Gottfried, 107.

5. Gottfried, 29.

6. Oscar G. Brockett and Robert R. Findlay, *Century of Innovation: A History of the European and American Theatre Since 1870* (Englewood Cliffs, N.J.: Prentice-Hall, 1973), 740-745.

7. Robert Pasolli, *A Book on the Open Theatre* (New York: Bobbs-Merrill, 1970), 2.

8. Martin Gottfried, *Opening Nights: Theatre Criticism of the Sixties* (New York: G. P. Putnam, 1969), 319.

9. Pasolli, 74.

10. Pasolli, 75.

11. Pasolli, 81.

12. Interview with Martin Gottfried, New York City, April 19, 1990.

Chapter 3

The Creation and Growth of *Hair*

First presented for a limited run at Joseph Papp's Public Theater on October 29, 1967, and after a brief engagement at the uptown discotheque, Cheetah, a completely revised, recast, and restaged *Hair* opened at the Biltmore Theatre on April 29, 1969. The date had been selected by Broadway producer Michael Butler's astrologer, Maria Elise Crummaire, who predicted that opening on that date would assure the venture's success. Her prognostications proved correct. *Hair* was the most successful musical of the season, and one of the most successful productions in the history of American musical theater.

How *Hair* got to Broadway is a dramatic story in itself, in which imagination, luck, and ingenuity converged. In this chapter, we shall follow *Hair*'s progress from Ragni and Rado's initial jottings to the preparations for it opening at the Biltmore.

HAIR'S CREATORS: RAGNI AND RADO

So natural and unified was *Hair* that many who attended its performances believed that it was truly a "happening" being created before their eyes. The piece delighted its audiences and enjoyed critical acclaim. Still, the Broadway establishment would have preferred that the piece remain in its downtown environs, out of sight, sound, and mind. Thus, the myth was created that *Hair* was the product of a bunch of hippies (authors, director, and actors) who had absolutely no theatrical background and no business being on Broadway. Although the creators had no deep or long-standing ties to the moneyed theater, the story that *Hair* arose from the streets by some sort of spontaneous generation is just a story. Giving the devil its due, *Hair*'s first director, Gerald Freedman, allowed that co-authors Gerome Ragni and James Rado were veteran actors when he met them in the fall of 1967, and that they shared a "wonderful theatrical sense."[1]

The two young men who wrote *Hair* had considerable background in the dramatic arts. A native of Pittsburgh, Gerome Ragni came to New York to realize his theatrical ambitions. He was a member of the Nola Chilton group that organized the Open Theatre in 1962-63, and in fact, he was the one who named the troupe.[2] Before he assumed the leading role of Berger in the Public Theater staging of *Hair*, Ragni had demonstrated his acting abilities in several successful off-Broadway shows, including *Hang Down Your Head and Die* and the long-running comedy *The Knack*. His Broadway credits included the John Gielgud-Richard Burton production of *Hamlet* (1964). In addition to his involvement in New York's experimental theater scene, Ragni had already begun to make a name for himself in off-Broadway and Broadway circles. Reminiscing about the early 1960s, noted theater critic Clive Barnes recalled that Ragni was "highly regarded" before *Hair* and that avant-garde director Peter Brook "was convinced that Ragni was a genius."[3]

Co-author James Rado had established even greater theater credentials before writing the rock musical and playing the part of Claude at the Biltmore. Hailing from Washington,

D.C., Rado first became involved in the dramatic arts while in college, where he wrote and played in several musical revues. Called a "consummate musician" by Ellen Stewart,[4] Rado had aspired to become a Broadway musical composer in the tradition of Rodgers and Hammerstein, Cole Porter, and other masters of the form even before he made his way to New York in the 1950s. Rado initially sought work as an actor in "legitimate" theater, but "got sidetracked" and began to write popular tunes with a rock flavor.[5] With one foot in the theater and the other in pop music, Rado's career stalled, and he was forced to do office work to support himself. Summer stock appearances in New Jersey kept his stage hopes alive, but it was only after joining Lee Strasberg's method acting classes that his career blossomed. In short order, Rado found himself in a succession of Broadway shows. First came June Havoc's *Marathon '33* produced by the Actors' Studio, followed by the Henry Fonda-led *Generation*, where he was Albert Finney's understudy in the title role of *Luther*, and, finally, in *The Lion in Winter*, he took a lead role playing opposite Rosemary Harris and Robert Preston.

COLLABORATION

It was in off-Broadway productions that "the boys," as Ellen Stewart affectionately calls them, met. The two actors formed a bond while playing in *Hang Down Your Head and Die* (a musical revue from London dealing with capital punishment) and began to appreciate one another's potential. The dream of collaborating to create a Broadway musical first took shape during their joint appearance in the Chicago company of *The Knack*. Through Ragni's influence, Rado was drawn into the world of experimental theater, and they both became excited about the new staging techniques that were evolving. Off-Broadway producer Eric Blau, who would

introduce composer Galt MacDermot to the *Hair* team, later
wrote of Ragni and Rado in the early 1960s that they were
unusual for New York actors of their day because of their
interest in the nature of theater far more than in their careers,
and in their knowledge of contemporary social and political
issues.[6] Blau also observed that "Jerry and Jim" were not
beatniks, freaks, or protohippies: they were clean-shaven,
closely-cropped, and ostensibly "straight" in mien.[7]

Through their activities in the downtown shows and acting
workshops, the authors were drawn to the long-haired youth
culture of Greenwich Village, with whom they shared antiwar
sentiments. Realizing that these young people, with their unconventional appearance, opposition to the war, and love of
rock music, embodied the stuff of theater, they began to
gather *Hair*'s raw material in early 1965, even before Fallon
had coined the term *hippie*. They continued their observations for the next two years. Using working methods akin to
that of the "participant/observer" procedures used in ethno-
graphic studies, they took to the streets of the Village and its
immediate environs where the hippies congregated. Compar-
ing their scribbled field notes at day's end, Ragni and Rado
confirmed their hunch about the latent power of their
"informants" as a source inspiration for musical theater.

As a member of the Open Theatre group, Ragni partici-
pated in *Viet Rock* workshops. On occasion he brought along
long-haired high school students that he had met in and
around MacDougal Street's Cafe Figaro. It was during these
sessions, he recalls, that "*Hair* really started to develop."[8] By
the time that *Viet Rock*'s run at LaMama ended, the hippie
population had grown and could be found in almost any
quarter of Manhattan—conducting protest marches on Fifth
Avenue, organizing happenings, be-ins and love-ins in
Central Park, or just plain "hanging out" on the sidewalks
that they inhabited. No longer limited to the Village, the
authors enlarged their area of concentration, taking more

notes, consolidating their findings. Their observations and explorations became the book and lyrics of *Hair*.

IN SEARCH OF A PRODUCER

By the middle of 1966, Ragni and Rado had crafted a script, which featured a social protest theme, a plot that revolved around a young man's indecision to go or not go to war, characters and scenes based on the hippie lifestyle, and verses to a dozen-odd songs. Their stage directions were explicitly experimental.

A rift in the Open Theatre group divided the members during the period of their appearances at LaMama. Some thought the company should remain exclusively a workshop. Others believed they should welcome opportunities offered by the outside theater. Sensitive to the situation, Ragni switched his affiliation to Robbins's American Theatre Laboratory. Opportunistically, he presented his co-authored work to Robbins, who met with Ragni and Rado on several occasions to discuss the script's narrative line and characters. Ragni recalls, "Robbins gave us wonderful advice and came up with very constructive criticism."[9]

Either on their own or through their literary agent, Janet Roberts, the authors began to shop their script from one Broadway producer to the next. Hal Prince read the script, and returned it with the inexplicable comment, "Dear Janet, what seems unconventional to you is extremely conventional." *Rejected*. The script found its way to Robert Whitehead's office. It was sent back with the more accurate appraisal that it was not Whitehead's "cup of tea." *Rejected*. They auditioned the songs for David Merrick's assistant Biff Liff, who loved MacDermot's score, and enthusiastically recommended the piece to his boss. "What's it about?" Merrick asked.

"Hippies," Liff replied. Merrick's replied, "Get out of here." *Rejected.*[10]

MEETING WITH PAPP

In September 1966, an Open Theatre production of *Viet Rock* was staged at Yale University. It initiated the season that began Robert Brustein's deanship at the Drama School. Ragni, who was a member of the cast, solicited the new dean's interest. Brustein read the piece and expressed his admiration, but he could not envision *Hair* as a one unit set, thought there were too many scene changes, and believed the production would be too costly. The university simply didn't have the funds to underwrite this otherwise worthy project.[11]

Quite by chance, on the train back to New York, Ragni met Joseph Papp, who was teaching a theater course on Shakespeare at Yale. Since the early 1950s, Papp had headed the yearly New York Shakespeare Festival, which offered free performances of the Bard's works in Central Park and elsewhere around the city. Aware of Papp's progressive theater sponsorship, Ragni approached him. Papp later recounted their intitial meeting. "I've just written something with Jimmy Rado, would you like to see it? . . . Well, it's kind of a musical called *Hair*." Ragni showed Papp six or eight handwritten pages. Papp read the material, and asked if Ragni had any more. "There are more pages at home, he answered."[12]

Ragni delivered the script to Papp the next morning. "On going through the rest of *Hair*, without the music, my reaction wandered all over the place," Papp says, "some of it was boring and some was interesting. The thing that struck me was that it had to do with the loneliness of young people, and that's why I became involved in the material."[13] Papp confirmed his interest. He got back to Ragni the very next day, stating the possibility of producing *Hair* at the old Astor Library that was being completely renovated into the Public Theater—with the proviso that they get a composer.[14]

MACDERMOT COMES ABOARD

In the course of their careers, Ragni and Rado had become acquainted with many members of New York's artistic community. Working with Isabelle Blau in the Chilton and Open Theatre workshops, Ragni had met Blau's then-husband, Eric, a musical theater producer. Going over the book with the authors, Blau agreed that further refinement of the project—the final setting of the lyrics—demanded a score. Rado had a musical background and had performed in a rock band, but his efforts to compose a score were not satisfactory. Blau suggested Galt MacDermot, a composer whom he had once considered. Through music publisher-manager Nat Shapiro, MacDermot joined the creative team. Shapiro became the team's manager.[15]

MacDermot had an interesting and somewhat unusual background. He was born in Montreal and educated at Capetown University in South Africa. In the late 1950s, his "African Waltz" was a smash hit in England, and it earned him a Grammy Award in the United States. A formally trained musician, he had composed in all kinds of idioms—jazz, pop, blues, country and western, as well as rock and roll. When he met Ragni and Rado, MacDermot was a jazz pianist at a local metropolitan club. He had never written for theater.

Blau's hunch clicked. MacDermot composed the tunes that would eventually be assessed as among the most captivating elements of the musical. He drew heavily on his knowledge of African rhythms to which he had been exposed as a child in South Africa to create the feeling of freedom for the show's lyrics. In composing the score, he explained that he was "trying to communicate the elements of freedom, a musical approach that I had learned in Africa, and which is really the basis of American music, and put it into the theater."[16] MacDermot reached down and heard the echoes of beats used by the Bantu people in their tribal rituals.[17] His working method was "to set the music," which he described as crystallized Ragni and Rado, "to the mentality of the poet and let the literal meaning of the words take care of itself."[18] MacDermot heard "the melodies of the Bantus" in his head, and the score was completed in two weeks.[19]

Auditions for prospective producers were held in a rehearsal hall on Forty-seventh Street. Eric Blau and his associate Henry Hoffman attended one of the first sessions. When they heard MacDermot at the piano and Ragni and Rado singing the score, they were convinced of the show's potential. Blau recounts that Hoffman left the auditions humming the tunes, and they quickly made an offer to produce *Hair* off-Broadway.[20] Blau and Hoffman would eventually stage their own off-Broadway musical hit, but it was *jacques brel is alive and well and living in paris*. The "fly in the ointment," as Blau would later see it, was Joseph Papp, who was also at the audition, equally impressed, and ready to make a commitment. Papp's contract offered a guaranteed engagement of eight weeks at a new and beautiful venue, whereas Blau and Hoffman could only guarantee the show would open.

Discussing the options with Ragni and Rado, Blau undercut his own proposal by telling them "to have the sponsorship of a new and important nonprofit theater organization, and to be its initial attraction was not to be resisted."[21] Ragni and Rado had always intended their piece for Broadway, but they accepted Papp's offer because of the anticipated press coverage, and because they were, in Rado's words, "eager to get it on."[22] A contract was inked, a schedule of rehearsals, previews, and performances devised, and *Hair* was on its way.

PAPP AND THE CHOICE OF A DIRECTOR

The reasons why Ragni and Rado accepted Joe Papp's offer are fairly straightforward. But, other than its inherent merits, why did Papp, more closely associated with Shakespearean drama, make his offer? To begin, Papp was in the organizational forefront of a new chapter in nonprofit theatrical history. The Public Theater was part of his larger vision for nonprofit theater in America. According to Clive Barnes, Papp was entering into his own "Age of Aquarius" with long-range plans to start a national theater.[23] The piece that opened the Public would long be remembered as such, and Papp wanted something revolutionary.

In explaining his selection of *Hair* for the first presentation at the Public Theater, Papp expressed his belief in its social relevance: "We must be a modern theatre, engaged in producing modern plays dramatizing the potent forces of our time—events and feelings which shape history and man."[24] Papp was struck by the vitality of the hippie counterculture which engulfed the East Village neighborhood in which the Public Theater was located. He was particularly drawn to the freshness, naivete, and sincerity of the group.[25]

Once the rights were secured, Papp called Ragni and Rado to inquire about their ideas for a director. The authors needed little time to ruminate. They had seen a performance of *Futz*, written by Rochelle Owens, at the original Cafe LaMama on Second Avenue. They wanted *Futz* director Tom O'Horgan, whom they had already approached with the idea.[26] Their friendships had already been kindled at LaMama, and they shared the same interests in the experimental theater of the time.

According to the authors, O'Horgan was already committed to take the LaMama troupe to Europe in the fall of 1967, and was therefore unavailable. However, Stewart alleges the real reason for O'Horgan's absence at the Public was that

Papp simply didn't want him. If he had expressed an interest, she would have guaranteed his availability.[27] In support of this account, Papp undoubtedly had been wary of O'Horgan's experimental leanings. Moreover, O'Horgan had never directed a musical. When queried as to a second choice, the authors suggested Chaikin. He was rejected because he was too social, too Brechtian.[28]

Actually, Papp had his own directorial preference in mind— Gerald Freedman, with whom he had been associated in the Shakespeare-in-the-Park series, and who was the Public's artistic director. His work on *The Taming of the Shrew*, *King Lear*, *Macbeth*, *Peer Gynt*, and *Hamlet* had earned him much critical approval. Like Papp, Freedman was interested in the hippie counterculture, and was convinced of *Hair*'s importance. "The flower culture, both alien and fascinating," he said, "was a particularly American phenomenon and it was happening all around the Public."[29] What he saw in the material was a "terrific vulnerability, a tremendous innocence, but a courage about what these kids were doing."[30]

Freedman was responsible for putting the playwrights' material into a form that was acceptable to the Public Theater. As critic Clive Barnes commented: "Yes, I'm absolutely sure that if Freedman had not done whatever he had done in the initial stage, it would never have gone anywhere. I suspect that the text that Freedman received was in a state that no one would have looked at it."[31]

Although the authors were theater people who had a "wonderful instinct for theatre," Freedman asserted that they had no instinct for form.[32] Freedman rearranged some scenes, deleted others, and gave the piece a narrative unity. Although the material seemed plotless, there was a muted linearity. Claude is drafted, goes to war, and is killed. While the characters had clear and definable differences, they were more archetypal. In Freedman's words: "the black boy, the goofball, the spacehead, the tough girl, the spacey girl, the little girl."[33] Lack of character was not considered a short-coming, because *Hair* was not about character, but about a lifestyle. The focus was on theme.[34] The downtown production, Freedman observed, was similar to the revues that dominated the American musical theater prior to *Show Boat*. It was a series of sketches on which musical numbers were clotheslined.[35]

Freedman believed in discipline and detail in the theater, so the challenge was how to create a sense of spontaneity and amateurishness in a professional context. There were many problems because he wanted to keep a show that had theatrical discipline. He had to devise various techniques that were new to him "to structure the piece, but at the same time keep it open, so that I wouldn't lose that kind of sense."[36] He used certain experimental techniques, improvisation, and organic blocking. Most notably, he used the three-sided arena stage to break the illusion of reality. The cast mingled with the audience, and handed flowers to the patrons at the end of the performance.

Freedman had been Jerome Robbins's assistant in *West Side Story*, and he was aware of the experimenting the director-choreographer was attempting. Robbins had already done *West Side Story* and *Fiddler on the Roof*, but there was still a conventional quality about his directorial approach.

Freedman's insistence on directorial control and theatrical discipline brought him into conflict with the authors. "It was their inability to understand that when you put on a show every night, after you've discovered what the piece should be through improvisation, it has to have a predictable beginning, middle, and end."[37]

The Broadway show lost some of its structure. The focus was no longer on understanding, or getting into the hippie lifestyle. It became more of a freak show in Freedman's estimation. He was trying to say, "Look at where these ideas are coming from, show how they evolved. These kids have feelings."[38] And the parents were portrayed by adults. They played up the conflict. The audience knew where the "kids were coming from."

THE SOKOLOW EPISODE

For the task of choreography, Papp again asked the authors their choice. This time their request was honored. Anna Sokolow also had been a member of Robbins's workshop. According to her official biographer, Larry Warren, Sokolow's attempts to instill an aura of professionalism brought her into conflict with some of the cast and crew. She believed that the nondancers needed close supervision and discipline.[39]

Even before *Hair*'s first public performance, Sokolow's tight rein created conflicts. She was at loggerheads with Freedman, who had his own ideas about how *Hair* should move. In the squabble, Freedman withdrew from the show for ten days, and Papp assigned the directing functions to Sokolow. However, her tenure in both roles was short-lived. After the first preview of *Hair*, an irate Papp called Ragni and Rado into his office. He was upset, among other things, with Sokolow's replacement of Walker Daniels in the leading role of Claude by Rado. An edict was issued. The show would be closed unless Daniels was brought back, Freedman reinstated, and Sokolow dismissed. The authors had little choice but to accede to the demands. With Sokolow gone, Freedman resumed his original command and became the dance director as well.[40]

According to Freedman, he "took out all the choreography that had been added" by Sokolow during his absence, because "it looked too choreographed, when the look should have been spontaneous."[41] Even after the cuts, Brustein wrote of the Public's choreography that it was "antithetical to an authentic hippie atmosphere which should be cool . . . other than bouncing with chorus boy energy."[42]

There was no mention of Anna Sokolow in the program on opening night. Julie Arenal, who had been Sokolow's assistant for several years, became the dance director at the Biltmore, and in the authors' opinion, Sokolow never received the credit she deserved: "A lot of Anna's work at the Public influenced the Broadway production."[43]

THE APPROACH AT THE PUBLIC

Hair was the first presentation to be staged at the Public, and its initial success helped to launch the theater as a major venue for innovative works.[44] Architect Giorgio Cavaglieri had fashioned a breathtaking showcase for their piece at the Anspacher Theater. The environment was so spacious and esthetically pleasing that one reviewer remarked that "an audience at the Public Theater is already half won before a play begins."[45] The location of the Public in the heart of the counterculture scene served to heighten the sense of the show's immediacy and authenticity.

Ming Cho Lee, a trusted member of Papp's ensemble was the set designer. According to one critic, his "striking and attractive" creation was superior to that of the Broadway production.[46] Lee began the tradition of using "real" hippie artifacts, objects, posters, and found objects, taken directly from head shops and hangouts in the Public's immediate vicinity, as props and stage elements. Theoni Aldredge, another Papp associate, had little difficulty as costume designer reproducing standard hippie attire.

Casting, however, presented a problem. The script called for a score of youthful actors to fill hippie parts, as well as two older figures to portray Claude's parents. Largely talented but unknown professionals were selected. Empathizing with Freedman's need to find the right balance between talent and "natural" hippie types, O'Horgan described *Hair*'s first cast as "conventional," implying that too much emphasis had been placed on the talent end of the scale.[47] Walker Daniels played Claude, Jill O'Hara assumed the role of Sheila, and as for the part of Berger, Freedman used co-author Ragni, stating that he "could not find anyone who better fit the role."[48] The secondary leads of Woof, Hud, Jeannie, and Crissy were handled respectively by Steve Dean, Arnold Wilkerson, Sally Eaton, and Shelley Plimpton. Commenting on the vocal abilities of the actors, MacDermot, as a true composer, later complained that other than Shelley Plimpton, "there wasn't one good singer" in the troupe.[49] (A complete list of the cast appears in Appendix A.)

As stated before, Freedman rearranged scenes, took out loose material, and put the original material into a coherent form. He tightened the book by deleting material not directly related to the antiwar movement and/or the storyline. Some of the songs and scenes he took out managed to find their way back into the Broadway production. Looking back, Freedman argues that, "the material that I took out never found its legs," it was merely "filler" that interfered with the "registering" of the important pieces.[50] Some of the livelier tunes, especially those with a strong rock impulse, were deleted. "I remember Jerry Freedman saying to me, 'but Galt, that's not theatrical,' " MacDermot recalls, confessing that he never really understood what the director intended by the word *theatrical*.[51] Even more subdued pieces came under the axe. Freedman initially wanted to eliminate the song "Frank Mills," which became a showstopper in both the downtown and uptown productions. He was dissuaded from doing so only after MacDermot's repeated urgings.[52]

With far fewer songs than would be heard at the Biltmore, the downtown show had a fuller narrative line, including the authors' plottings of a *Jules and Jim*-type *ménage-à-trois* motif among the three leads. Contrasting the Public and the Biltmore productions, Martin Gottfried says of the former that, "it was a regular book musical," with a "corny, but nevertheless, cogent story," much of which would be excoriated by the authors and Broadway director O'Horgan.[53]

THE SHOW CLOSES AT THE PUBLIC

"During the entire eight week run, the cast hardly knew what was going on . . . or what to expect,"[54] Ragni said of the clashes occurring backstage. Sokolow's dismissal and the tug-of-war between Freedman, Ragni, and Rado over the show's production restraints were not the only conflicts to erupt within the company. A feud arose between the authors and Papp on the issue of further revisions to the script. During previews and performances, Ragni and Rado had continued in their process of refining the show to write new material. Their suggested revisions, delivered to the producer in memo form, were returned in shreds. There were to be no revisions. The piece had been set.

When *Hair* closed, Papp was attending to the next production in his subscription series, and expressed no interest in a transfer to Broadway. Just when it seemed that *Hair* would be permanently consigned to the marginal file of unusual theater pieces that had once played off-Broadway, not one, but two wild cards were added to the deck.

Michael Butler, a youthful scion of the exceedingly wealthy, Chicago-based Butler family, who had already invested with Roger Stevens in *West Side Story* and *The Golden Apple*, was in New York with Governor Otto Kerner of the Kerner Commission on Civil Disobedience to meet with Mayor John Lindsay. Butler had worked with John and Robert Kennedy. As a decidedly liberal candidate, he had political aspirations of his own, and had acquitted himself well as the Democratic party's representative in an Illinois election. (He lost narrowly in a traditionally Republican bastion.) The mistreatment of the American Indians was one of Butler's concerns. He wanted to get involved with the Bureau of Indian Affairs.[55]

Sitting at the New York Racquet Club between meetings, Butler noticed an advertisement in the *New York Times* for *Hair*, the American Tribal Love-Rock Musical. The logo featured a "very famous Indian photograph of Geronimo, Sitting Bull, and a couple of other chiefs" (which happened to be superimposed photographs of Ragni and Rado). "My God," he reacted, "the Indians have put a show together." He got tickets to the first preview and saw the show with his friend Olivier Coquelin, who owned a couple of discotheques in New York, one of which was the Cheetah.[56] There were no Indians, but neither of them were disappointed.

"I fell in love with the show," Butler says, "mainly because I was getting ready to run for the Senate against Dirksen, with both Daly's and Kerner's blessings. And I thought I'd like to take the show back to Illinois to show my constituents what I thought of the Vietnam War."[57]

A "progressive" politician, Butler was adamantly opposed to the American involvement in Vietnam. He was also a self-styled free spirit who strongly identified with the mystical and communal qualities of the hippies being portrayed at the Public. Immediately after the show, Butler called old friend Roger Stevens to arrange a meeting with Papp to inquire about a joint venture on Broadway. Papp replied that he "intended just to run the show for a few weeks, as was the case with rep shows, and then just close it down."[58]

Once positive reviews starting amassing, however, Papp got back to Butler, expressing a guarded interest in co-producing the show at a larger house. The Broadway partnership never materialized, but it did open the door for Butler, in conjunction with Bertrand Castelli, to secure the first class rights, which Papp let expire. Yet the Public was to share in the Broadway profits, which Butler says, "kept them running for years."[59] Called a dream producer by Ragni and Rado,

Butler allowed the artistic freedom necessary to potentiate their vision of *Hair*.

Butler characterized his soon-to-be partner this way: "Bertrand was that mysterious, crazy showman who you saw in the sixties, the guy with the business suit and the beads."[60] Castelli was a writer-producer of considerable repute in Parisian art circles where he rubbed elbows with the first-rank creative personalities of this century: Picasso, Raoul Dufy, Jean Cocteau, and Colette. His activities bridged the gap between the classical and the avant-garde. At the time of *Hair*'s Public Theater staging, Castelli was the director of the Harkness Ballet. In his role as ballet impresario, he brought in a number of "experimentalists," including Andy Warhol and Tom O'Horgan, to inject vitality into the "precious, static, obsolete world of ballet."[61]

Castelli was vehemently opposed to the war (he would later produce a film against Nixon), and he saw backing the show as a ready-made way to accelerate the goals of the antiwar movement. Castelli also detected an existential undertone in *Hair*, later stating that he felt the "whole piece was a reflection of what Sartre said or what Picasso painted," the essence of the "generation of children who were born from Picasso's dream, from Sartre's anguish."[62] Not many others would accord the same depth of interpretation, but for the "crazy showman," *Hair* was an integral step in the march of post-World War II culture, and he quickly signed on as *Hair*'s executive producer.

THE CHEETAH PRODUCTION

Butler and Castelli both knew Olivier Coquelin, who accompanied each of his friends to separate Public Theater performances. Butler had already realized that even though Papp would be involved with the show technically until the rights ran out through its transfer to the Cheetah, Papp was not going to become involved in a co-production on Broadway. He also realized that, even though the project was already fully capitalized, Broadway theater owners were not going to make a house available for the production.

At Coquelin's suggestion, in late December 1967 *Hair* was moved lock, stock, cast, and props to the Cheetah (Forty-fifth Street and Broadway), where it had 45 performances. The Cheetah had a capacity of nearly 700, as compared to the Public's 300, so wider exposure and larger receipts were projected. William Goldman saw the transfer as an "astute idea," the youth-oriented discotheque being the "perfect place to unite this show about the kids and their troubles with kids who have troubles."[63] Drawn primarily by Papp's reputation, most of the audiences at the Public had been older, middle class types. The Cheetah crowd was significantly younger and "hipper." In the turned-on *palais de danse*, the cast felt at home and mingled freely with the disco-audiences. The presence of the *Hair* people on the dance floor before and after the show contributed to the absence of "any fourth wall feeling whatsoever."[64]

As a temporary way-station, the Cheetah served its purpose, but as the show's permanent abode, it left much to be desired. The anticipated fusion of the theatergoers and the disco crowd did not happen. The Cheetah's acoustics were absolutely terrible for a theatrical presentation. The set was cavernous, and the stage was too close to the front row seats. Julie Arenal (and/or Tom O'Horgan) had not yet been enlisted to revise *Hair*'s choreography, and the Sokolow-Freedman dance movements seemed all the more like cliché-ridden production numbers when seen alongside the improvisations of the patrons performing the latest disco steps.[65] On top of these technical drawbacks, the Cheetah show was a commercial disaster. As Castelli allows, the producers were forced to close the show because "moneywise, we could not survive there."[66] A disenchanted Butler called his father to apprise him of misgivings about a venture that should have been a "sure-fire" hit. The father advised, "fish or cut bait, drop the turkey, or go the route and take *Hair* to Broadway."[67]

ENTER O'HORGAN

Butler maintains that he wanted to see changes in the production before transferring it uptown, and actually welcomed Papp's decision not to follow through as the show's co-producer. Butler was dissatisfied with Freedman and his direction. "As good as he was," Butler would say of *Hair*'s first director, "he never smoked grass." To Butler, Freedman was more of a "negative-minded" beatnik than an exuberant hippie. In particular, Butler was convinced that Freedman's staged ending for *Hair* at the Public (six toy tanks blasting away at the audience, with no hope for redemption) was a "downer" that would never sell to a mass audience.[68]

Yet, Ragni and Rado report that Michael Butler was entirely satisfied with the Public Theater production of *Hair*. As a matter of fact, he fought the authors on their adamant demands for refinements. The co-authors recalled, "When Butler told us he wanted to move the Cheetah show to Broadway, we said, 'Nothing doing. You're not moving this production to Broadway. We're rewriting the script. We want it recast, a new set designer, and a new director.' "[69] Butler said no, and they parted ways.

Hearing nothing from Butler for over a month, the authors started auditioning again at the Harlequin Studios for Biff Liff, Arthur Cantor, and other producers. They finally got a call from Butler, who said he wanted to do it. He asked who they wanted as director. They replied: Tom O'Horgan.

Hair underwent a massive overhaul between its closing at the Cheetah in January 1968 and its opening at the Biltmore three months later. Some thirteen new songs were written. The band was enlarged to include more brass and greater amplification, and Ragni and Rado finally got their way—O'Horgan was signed to direct. The authors had an ally in Bertrand Castelli, who shared their conviction that O'Horgan was the man to fill the directorial bill. O'Horgan was at his peak when he was asked to direct *Hair* on Broadway.[70] And in the view of Ellen Stewart and others, it was Tom O'Horgan, more than anyone else, who made *Hair* work at the Biltmore.[71]

The idea of taking *Hair* to Broadway had a special appeal for O'Horgan. He was convinced that Broadway and its audiences needed to be revitalized by a powerful dose of experimental theatrics. In the Biltmore souvenir program, he explained: "I took this assignment because I feel *Hair* is an assault on the theatrical dead area: Broadway. It's almost an effort to give Broadway mouth-to-mouth resuscitation."[72] Properly schooled, O'Horgan brought to Broadway the entire gamut of his avant-garde repertoire in staging his version of *Hair*.

O'Horgan occupied the same elevated stance in Stewart's experimental pantheon as director-theorist Jerzy Grotowski, who Stewart brought to New York from his native Poland. Both were at LaMama at the same time, and in the Mama's words, "It just so happens that these two masters were on the same track at the same time. Tom did not get his spirituality or his insight or anything at all from Grotowski."[73]

O'Horgan had come from Second City. Part of the exploratory thinking of the time, he was in tune with Grotowski's techniques, to which he would add an encounter group sensibility. He was awarded the 1967 Obie for best off-off-Broadway director of the year, as well as the 1968 Brandeis Award for Creative Arts, and *Cue* magazine called him the "high priest of off-Broadway." He had directed *Tom Paine* at Stage 73, but was most frequently acclaimed for his direction of outstanding productions at Cafe LaMama. He had just staged Rochelle Owen's *Futz* (an absurdist parable about a farmer's love for his pig), a show that received critical plaudits in America and abroad. *Newsweek* later called O'Horgan 1968's "Director of the Year," owing to his part in *Hair* at the Biltmore.[74] Four years later, James Huffman said that O'Horgan "more than anybody else is responsible for the injection of the counterculture into the moneyed theatre."[75] Samuel Leiter, in his *Ten Seasons: New York Theatre in the Seventies*, placed O'Horgan among the talents of Bob Fosee, Gower Champion, Harold Prince, and Michael Bennett who found success in the concept musical vernacular that marked the Broadway of the seventies.[76]

O'Horgan shared with the other creative team members a regard for *Hair*'s social relevance. For him theater was "the conscience and the morality of the people," and he saw *Hair* as a "once in a lifetime" opportunity to help create "a theatre form whose demeanor, language, clothing, dance, and even its name accurately reflect a social epoch in full explosion."[77]

THE TEAM ASSEMBLES AND SEARCHES
FOR A THEATER

Robin Wagner, who had been at the Harkness with Castelli, was enlisted as scenic designer. His stage credits included the Lincoln Center productions of *Galileo* and *The Condemned of Altona*, plus *The Trial of Lee Harvey Oswald*, *In White America*, and *A View From the Bridge*. In turn, Wagner contacted lighting expert Jules Fisher, whose recent credits included *Black Comedy*, *You Know I Can't Hear You When the Water's Running*, and *Scuba-Duba*. Julie Arenal had previously choreographed for Theatre Company of Boston, and for Harvard's Loeb Dance Center. She had also "worked closely with Sokolow for several years, sometimes as her assistant."[78] From New York's APA Phoenix Repertory Company, *Hair* sought Nancy Potts, who was the costume designer for *You Can't Take It With You*, *War and Peace*, and *Pantagleize*. The artistic crew was assembled, but the search for a theater continued.

The downtown production had been somewhat of a compromise for the authors who envisioned their project on Broadway. After the Cheetah closing, however, *Hair* headed downtown once more to the Ukrainian Hall in the East Village. Recast for its Broadway reincarnation under O'Horgan's direction, the show went into rehearsals, which were attended by prospective theater owners. The Shuberts came down, as did the Nederlanders and other Broadway theater owners. "They didn't like what they saw and heard, and none of them were willing to take the risk."[79] For a time, the show was effectively back where it started before Ragni's fateful meeting with Papp on the train from New Haven. This time, Castelli pulled the strings. He met with Michael Butler's father, a man who had strong political clout. Through the intervention of the senior Butler, personal friend and theater owner David Cogan was convinced to make the Biltmore available for the show that would rock Broadway.[80]

THE BROADWAY *HAIR*

Described in detail in the next chapter, the Broadway version was a far cry from its Public or Cheetah forerunners. It was completely revised, rewritten, recast, and restaffed. The authors wrote new material, notably thirteen new songs in collaboration with MacDermot. Issues that were forbidden now became permissible under the new regime. O'Horgan made excellent use of the rehearsal period during which much improvisational innovation to evolved from a new set of cast members. Other experimental staging techniques, which focused heavily on production elements tied to the theme of the hippie lifestyle, were intensely advanced, and Broadway's first fully realized concept musical emerged.

According to O'Horgan, the show changed radically during the rehearsal period. The boys were there working.

Songs and scenes were written on the spot. He recalls that
" 'What a Piece of Work Is Man' was written practically
during the rehearsal."[81] The extent of the revision is reflected
in the deletions, additions, and sequence changes of the songs
which appear in the programs at the Public and at the Biltmore. See the following lists.

THE PUBLIC THEATER SONG SEQUENCE

Act I

Red, Blue, and White	Mom and Dad
Ain't Got No	Claude, Berger, Woof, and Company
I Got Life	Claude and Mom
Air	Jeannie, Crissy, Dionne
Going Down	Berger and Company
Hair	Claude, Berger, and Company
Dead End	Sheila and Company
Frank Mills	Crissy
Where Do I Go	Claude and Company

Act II

Electric Blues	Suzannah, Linda, Paul
Easy to Be Hard	Suzannah, Linda, Paul, and Company
Manchester	Claude
White Boys	Dionne, Susan, Alma
Black Boys	Linda, Crissy, Suzannah
Walking in Space	Company
Aquarius	Company
Good Morning Starshine	Sheila and Company
Exanaplanetooch	Claude, Sheila
Climax	Sheila

THE BILTMORE THEATRE SONG SEQUENCE

Act I

Aquarius	Ron and Company
Donna	Berger and Company

Hashish	Company
Sodomy	Woof and Company
Colored Spade	Hud and Company
Manchester	Claude and Company
Ain't Got No	Company
I Believe in Love	Sheila
Air	Jeanie, Crissy, Dionne, and Company
Initials	Company
I Got Life	Claude and Company
Going Down	Berger and Company
Hair	Claude, Berger, and Company
My Conviction	Tourist Lady
Easy to Be Hard	Sheila
Don't Put It Down	Berger, Steve, and Woof
Frank Mills	Crissy
Be-In	Company
Where Do I Go	Claude and Company

Act II

Electric Blues	Suzannah, Leata, Steve, and Paul
Black Boys	Martha, Suzannah, and Natalie
White Boys	Dionne, Lorrie, and Emmaretta
Walking in Space	Company
Abie Baby	Hud, Ron, Tommy, and Lorrie
Three-Five-Zero-Zero	Company
Good Morning Starshine	Sheila, Dionne, and Company
The Bed	Company
Aquarius (reprise)	Company
Ain't Got No (reprise)	Claude
Manchester (reprise)	Claude
Eyes Look Your Last	Company
The Flesh Failures (Let the Sun Shine In)	Claude, Sheila, Dionne, and Company

Summarizing the changes one notes:

1. Act I at the Public contains nine songs, compared to the nineteen at the Biltmore. The number of songs in Act II remains constant at ten.

2. Thirteen new songs appear in the Broadway version. Most were newly written. Some represent those deleted at the Public.

3. Three numbers ("Dead End," "Exanaplanetooch," and "Climax") from the Public version are deleted from the Broadway version.

4. Changes in the sequence of songs occur. Most significantly, the opening number downtown—"Red, Blue, and White"—appears later in the first act at the Biltmore, entitled "Don't Put It Down." The Biltmore version opens with "Aquarius."

Many of the added songs extended the show's thematic concerns with the war in Vietnam and racial injustice, but the Broadway *Hair* took on new pro-love, pro-sex, pro-drugs, and other antiestablishment causes, as the meaning of the hippie phenomenon was construed more broadly than at the Public.[82] In Freedman's view, the substitution of "Aquarius" for "Don't Put It Down" was emblematic of a shift from the show's original preoccupation with the war to greater emphasis on the "tribal" nature of the hippies.[83] The tribe's members at the Public were hippies because they opposed the war. At the Biltmore, they opposed the war because they were hippies.

With more songs to fill the same two-and-a-half-hour showtime slot, the narrative elements were deemphasized. The result was "a decimated version of the already plotless story told earlier downtown."[84] *Hair* at the Biltmore had become "a succession of songs and dances with [almost] no libretto to absorb any of the time."[85] The book, in the traditional sense, was all but banished from the Biltmore production. Emphasis was not on plot, character, or theme, but on picturesque physical activity and bold anti-illusionistic devices. The tribe's ensemble subsumed any individuality of character once more, but there was a noticeable difference in the portrayal of Claude's parents. Originally played by two adult actors, they were played in triplicate in the Broadway production. Three young female actresses played the three "dads," and three young male actors played the three "moms" in drag. In the Biltmore version, the "parent generation" was deprived of a legitimate viewpoint within the show, and became mere butts of the tribe's comic antics.[86] Rado freely admits that in the Broadway treatment, the parents "were definitely less sympathetic, more comical."[87] In O'Horgan's version, no attempt was made to give the "parent generation" its moment as an alternative representation to the hippies; rather, they became mere mockeries, as any other authoritary figure.

The spirit of the show changed. As the polemic against society was undercut, it became permeated with the hippie cult.[88] Butler endorsed this viewpoint, stating that "the Papp production was a much stronger antiwar statement . . . a real downer."[89] Freedman countered that on Broadway, *Hair* resembled a "freak show" or a "hippie happening."[90] In all accounts, the uptown *Hair* was stridently antiwar, climaxing with Claude's death, albeit followed by the joyously transcendent strains of "The Flesh Failures" and "Let the Sun Shine In." And the representational approach accorded the Freedman production gave way to the deliberate presentational theatrics manifested in the off-off-Broadway experimental scene from whence O'Horgan originated.

NOTES

1. Interview with Gerald Freedman, New York City, April 10, 1990.

2. Interview with Gerome Ragni, New York City, March 3, 1990.

3. Interview with Clive Barnes, New York City, April 19, 1990.

4. Interview with Ellen Stewart, New York City, May 15, 1990.

5. Interview with James Rado, New York City, March 11, 1990.

6. Eric Blau, *jacques brel is alive and well and living in paris* (New York: E. P. Dutton, 1971), 45.

7. Blau, 45.

8. Ragni interview.

9. Ragni interview.

10. Ragni interview.

11. Ragni interview.

12. Howard Greenberger, *The Off-Broadway Experience* (New York: Harcourt, Brace & World, 1969), 87.

13. Greenberger, 87.

14. Ragni interview.

15. Ragni interview.

16. Interview with Galt MacDermot, New York City, August 11, 1980.

17. Nahma Sandrow, "What Will *Hair* Say to the 70s?" *The New York Times* (October 1977): D26.

18. *Hair*, Biltmore Souvenir Program.

19. Biltmore Souvenir Program.

20. Biltmore Souvenir Program.

21. Blau, 46-47.

22. Ragni interview.

23. Barnes interview.

24. *The New York Shakespeare Festival Program*, 1967.

25. William Harris, "Theatre: A Man for All Seasons," *East Side Express* (October 27, 1977): 9.

26. Rado interview.

27. Stewart interview.

28. Ragni interview.

29. Interview with Greald Freedman, New York City, October 27, 1977.

30. Freedman interview, 1977.

31. Barnes interview.

32. Interview with Gerald Freedman, New York City, April 10, 1990.

33. Freedman interview, 1990.

34. Freedman interview, 1990.

35. Freedman interview, 1977.

36. Freedman interview, 1977.

37. Freedman interview, 1990.

38. Freedman interview, 1977.

39. Correspondence with Larry Warren, Ph.D., University of Maryland, Department of Dance, College Park, Maryland, March 9, 1990.

40. Warren interview.

41. Freedman interview, 1977.

42. Robert Brustein, "From *Hair* to *Hamlet*," *New Republic* (November 18, 1967): 39.

43. Rado interview.

44. Stuart W. Little, *Off-Broadway: The Prophetic Theater* (Englewood, N.J.: Prentice-Hall, 1971), 257.

45. Gerald Weales, "I Left It at the Astor," *Reporter* (April 4, 1968): 36.

46. George Oppenheimer, "On Stage," *The Newark Evening News* (June 8, 1968).

47. Interview with Tom O'Horgan, New York City, April 13, 1990.

48. Rado interview.

49. MacDermot interview, 1980.

50. Freedman interview, 1990.

51. Interview with Galt MacDermot, New York City, June 29, 1990.

52. MacDermot interview, 1990.

53. Interview with Martin Gottfried, New York City, April 19, 1990.

54. Ragni interview.

55. Interview with Michael Butler, New York City, April 3, 1990.

56. Butler interview.

57. Butler interview.

58. Butler interview.

59. Butler interview.

60. Craig Unger, *Blue Blood: How Rebekah Harkness, One of the Richest Women in the World, Destroyed a Great American Family* (New York: William Morrow, 1988), 145.

61. Unger, 145.

62. Interview with Bertrand Castelli, New York City, March 6, 1990.

63. William Goldman, *The Season: A Candid Look at Broadway* (New York: Harcourt, Brace & World, 1969), 381.

64. Goldman, 382.

65. Ronald Gold, "It's 'Non-Choreography,' But All Dance," *Dance Magazine* (July 1968): 29.

66. Castelli interview.

67. Collette Dowling, "How *Hair* Found Fortune and Fame," *Playbill* (September 1968): 35.

68. Butler interview.

69. Interview with Gerome Ragni and James Rado, New York City, March 3, 1990.

70. Gottfried interview.

71. Stewart interview.

72. Biltmore Souvenir Program.

73. Stewart interview.

74. "Director of the Year," *Newsweek* (June 3, 1968): 102.

75. James R. Huffman, "*Jesus Christ Superstar*—Popular Art and Unpopular Criticism," *Journal of Popular Culture* 6, no. 2 (Fall 1976): 264.

76. Samuel Leiter, *Ten Seasons: New York Theatre in the Seventies* (Westport, Ct.: Greenwood Press, 1986), 102.

77. Lorrie Davis and Rachel Gallagher, *Letting Down My Hair* (New York: Arthur Fields, 1973), 12.

78. Warren interview.

79. Castelli interview.

80. Castelli interview.

81. O'Horgan interview.

82. Abe Laufe, *Broadway's Greatest Musicals* (New York: Funk & Wagnalls, 1969), 358.

83. Freedman interview, 1990.

84. Gerald Bordman, *American Musical Theatre: A Chronicle* (New York: Oxford University Press, 1978), 657.

85. Martin Gottfried, *Opening Nights: Theater Criticism of the Sixties* (New York: G. P. Putnam, 1969), 103.

86. Goldman, 395.

87. Rado interview.

88. John Elson, *The Erotic Theatre* (New York: Taplinger Press, 1973), 203.

89. Butler interview.

90. Freedman interview, 1990.

Chapter 4

Hair on Broadway

While *Hair* at the Public overflowed from the three-sided arena and up the aisles in its attempt to involve the audience, this physical breakthrough was intensified on Broadway under O'Horgan's direction. The tribe entered back and forth through the audience, running and tumbling in the aisles, stepping on the backs of seats between the patrons in the orchestra, leaping on and off the stage, singing in the aisles, and swinging over the audience's heads on ropes. Berger (Gerome Ragni), clad in a hippie-Indian loincloth, began his opening monologue into the foot mike downstage center and ended it sitting in a woman's lap in the third row, asking for a handout. *Hair* broke the illusion of fourth wall reality. It was the authors' intent, and in their words, O'Horgan was the perfect one to do it.[1]

Hair was moved to a nonmusical Broadway house, and when the actors came down the aisles the audience was very much aware of the artifice and theatricality. As O'Horgan contended, the venerable, plush Biltmore contrasted nicely with the performance on the stage. The show had a very specific point of view. It really belonged in one of those "old plaster palaces where this group of people . . . this show was really out of its idiom. Hanging clothes and junk all over the festoons, actors scampering up and down the aisles, hanging all over the proscenium arch like really rebellious kids, that's what it was all about."[2]

The idea of staging *Hair* on Broadway had special appeal for O'Horgan, who saw the assignment as an assault on a theatrically dead area. "It's almost an attempt to give Broadway mouth-to-mouth resuscitation," he stated in the Biltmore souvenir program. While off-Broadway techniques were innovative, he observed that they were not being viewed by the establishment audiences who had become very comfortably accustomed to the theatrical conventions of Broadway. "It was time," he stated, "to seek out a larger and essentially unconvinced audience and purposefully turn their heads in a new direction."[3]

O'HORGAN'S EXPERIMENTAL TECHNIQUES

If there is a single word that expresses the directorial approach of Tom O'Horgan it is "unconventional." O'Horgan turned away from the stage conventions that had dominated Western theater for centuries and that no longer seemed relevant. Abandoning the traditional proscenium arch theater, he searched for new forms of expression in theater's holy ritual roots. O'Horgan believes in total theater with active involvement and participation by the audience. His theater is Artaudian: sensual, savage, and in the case of *Hair*, totally musical. In his productions, "manner tends to be more important than matter, since primary emphasis is placed not on story, character, or idea but on picturesque physical activity (writhing pantomines, subtextual business, human pyramids, and sexual semiexhibitionism), tableaux, bold anti-illusionistic devices, frantic light effects, amplified music and sound, and gimmickry of various sorts."[4]

O'Horgan believed in giving his actors as much latitude as possible in creating their roles. Somewhat similar to that of Jerzy Grotowski, his approach relied on extreme permissive-ness based on exploratory improvisation. He used a series of acting exercises that he had culled from the Esalen Institute for Human Potential and the Polish Lab Theatre designed to break down barriers between cast and crew. Based on exploratory touching, intensive examination, and attentive listening, these sensitivity exercises sought to increase the actor's awareness of others as human beings rather than as mere objects—to foster a mutual trust and understanding essential to ensemble work. Physical interaction and intimacy was combined with psychic bonding. For example, actors were asked to leap from a platform into the linked arms of fellow cast members. These exercise sessions continued throughout the Broadway run.

O'Horgan's approach to character was seen as unorthodox. Actors did not embody character in the traditional manner, which invited audience identification. Roles were fragmented, the cast was used as a chorus, and frequently actors moved from one role to another in a series of transformations, as dictated by the context. O'Horgan hoped these alienation techniques would help the actors to establish a critical objectivity, thereby clarifying the character's function. Actors were asked not to pretend to be the characters in the play so much as to present the essence of their roles while not losing sight of their personal identities. Coming from Second City, O'Horgan was also influenced by the "games" and role playing theories of human behavior as adapted to theater by Viola Spolin and Paul Sills. During rehearsals, a series of improvised games encouraged freedom and spontaneity. O'Horgan wanted his cast to be interchangeable, informing them that his "game" was for no one to know who he or she was playing in the show. Picking a part out of a hat required the cast to be well-versed on the entire show. While the issue was not forced, frequent role changes did occur. Melba Moore, an original black tribe member, took over the leading role of Sheila, who was very blonde and very white. Tribe member Robert I. Rubinsky stepped into the role of

Mom with balloons for bosoms; and black tribe member
Lorrie Davis played the part of Abraham Lincoln, a role she
created in rehearsals.[5] While some of the interchanges were
theatrically purposeful, others were a response to the chronic
absenteeism that later plagued the show. At one performance, Davis recalled, only two of the five leads showed up,
leaving sixteen of the tribe, mostly understudies, to carry the
show designed for a cast of twenty-five.[6]

CASTING

Casting presented a problem. O'Horgan wanted to pre-
serve the amateur quality common to experimental groups.
Thus, he sought talented individuals who had never performed on stage, but who could sing, and dance and perform
acrobatics. It was difficult in the beginning. "Nobody knew
exactly what we wanted at that point," recalls O'Horgan.
"Agents submitted people, actors, who had done glossy print
work, and then sang Noel Coward songs. It was very
strange."[7] Casting sessions were held for a long time, and the
creators saw literally thousands of individuals. Ragni and
Rado scoured the streets and subterranean clubs in search of
likely long-haired candidates. In the end they went to "places
where you wouldn't ordinarily look for people in a Broadway
show."[8]

Casting continued into the twenty-third day of rehearsals,
fifteen days before the first public performance, and "they
continued to cast twelve days after we opened."[9] Diane
Keaton had just graduated from the Neighborhood Playhouse. Melba Moore, a backup singer (and music teacher in
Newark), was discovered in a recording session. She had
never acted before. Lorrie Davis, also a gospel singer, had
danced at an exhibit at the World's Fair, and had limited
acting experience in television commercials. Suzannah
Norstrand was still attending the High School of the

Performing Arts. Toward the end, "we desperately started chasing people down the street who looked right for the parts."[10] Contrary to statements made by the press that O'Horgan had encouraged a bunch of "mainly hippie" performers to explore their own natures with song and dance, there were only "two" tribe members who were actually hippies. Both were female.[11]

What the cast had in common, aside from raw talent, was youth. Joseph Campbell Butler, a former member of the Lovin' Spoonful rock group, who took over the role of Claude when Rado left to appear in the Los Angeles production, remarked that he was amazed by the fact they were "just kids," many of whom were underage. In fact, young Ronnie Dyson was escorted to and from the Biltmore every night by his protective parents.[12]

Casting turned out to be an ongoing affair, as cast members moved to other roles within the production, went into other *Hair* companies as they sprang up across the country, or some simply dropped out of the theater scene entirely. Others moved to prominent roles in productions other than *Hair*. Tribe member Diane Keaton took over the role as Sheila before going into Woody Allen's *Play It Again, Sam*; tribe member Melba Moore replaced Heather MacRae as Sheila, and then went into the gospel musical *Purlie*. The multitalented Ben Vereen, who started as a tribe member in Los Angeles, worked his way up to the part of Hud in both the Los Angeles and New York shows and then left for the Judas role in *Jesus Christ Superstar*, going on from there to be voted Best Actor for his leading role in *Pippin*.

Absenteeism was another variable in the casting equation, as was the debilitating use of drugs. But the crucial factor, as Joe Butler sees it, was burnout.[13] *Hair* was an exceedingly taxing show, and even with the weeky injections of speed provided by the management, many members of the tribe were ill-equipped to endure the physical and mental strains inherent in the show.

As O'Horgan was not concerned with naturalism, he didn't need actors trained in traditional technique. These kids could sing and dance and perform acrobatics, but they had no stage experience. While some of the cast were truly gifted, they weren't professional. "They hadn't studied, they didn't have the underpinnings, any technique to fall back on. To do it every time, to believe it every time, eight times a week . . . it was hard."[14]

Amateurs, nonetheless, they were on Broadway, determined to make every performance their best. And they were terribly committed. "We cared," says Butler, "We had the luxury of being artists, so we could care." Over a door in the theater lobby was a sign that changed nightly, indicating the number of people that had been killed to date in Vietnam. It was all very meaningful. There was a change at the end of the show where Claude goes from hippie to dead soldier: "Backstage the wardrobe people would wop down your hair with stuff, velcro off your clothes, velcro on the army suit. You'd come on, and the line was: Berger, I feel like I died. And you sang, *Flesh Failures*. I used to get goose bumps, shaking, tears would roll down my cheeks when I sang it, because it reminded me of my own wasted time in the Air Force, before I'd joined the cast of *Hair*."[15]

Butler recalls that *Hair* was a terribly strenuous show. "It was a workout. I dumped weight. There was a lot of action . . . lot of moving . . . lot of energy. I was very strong. No, I didn't take the 'niacin.' I had been a drummer. I had about as much energy as anybody, but it was a number. As the kids (the cast) would say, 'Man, I've been working hard for the money.' "[16]

At the conclusion of the show, as an encore, Butler would slide on his knees forty feet across the stage. He didn't use kneepads. "They had to take forty cc's of fluid out of one knee. I was black and blue," he laughingly recalls. "And you had to be careful with your vocal cords." He spoke to other musical actors, like Jerry Orbach. "How do you do this night after night, those two days when you do it twice, without going totally bonkers? Without blowing your voice right out the window? Your lungs out through your nose?'' The veteran actor offered this advice, '' 'You never give them everything. You always hold back, never strain. This creates the illusion of how effortless it is, and then the audiences think, 'Wow, how great he is.' ''[17]

It was very much a milestone in Joe Butler's life to be a part of *Hair*, and he affectionately remembers the wonderful moments. Yet, he could not believe that *Hair* had become his life. He lived it, breathed it, and even dreamed about it. Illusion merged inextricably with reality. And even with his night club experience, he left the show after four months ''just beat to death.''[18]

THE BILTMORE CAST

A complete listing of the opening night Biltmore staff and cast appears in Appendix B. There were many replacements. Ragni continued to play the role of Berger. Encouraged by O'Horgan, Rado, who had been aching to get in the show, took over as Claude. Lynn Kellog replaced off-Broadway's Sheila. Shelly Plimpton and Sally Eaton continued their portrayals of Crissy and Jeanie, respectively. Steve Curry became the new Woof, Lamont Washington the new Hud. Cast changes in the minor parts underscored the emphasis on song and dance. The casting of Rado in the role of Claude caused a bit of critical consternation; although reportedly in his early thirties, the actor acquitted himself well as a character in his teens or early twenties. Yet it was charismatic Ragni as the kinetic Berger who penetrated the audience's psyche. Cast member Lorrie Davis, by no means a fan of either of the authors, gave the ''psychedelic teddy bear''[19] his due: his energy was contagious, his performances, sensational.[20]

THE REHEARSAL-WORKSHOP PERIOD

Much of *Hair* was crafted out of the collaborative contributions during rehearsal improvisations. The discovery process was most important to the piece. The rehearsal-workshop period was a time when, "Tom, and Jim, and Jerry, everybody could really work on the play and let it evolve, in an organic way."[21]

Rather than entering the rehearsal period with set ideas, O'Horgan allowed the cast, many of whom had never been in a Broadway theater, to explore their own personalities, encouraging their contributions to the final work. So great was the collective contribution, a tribute to O'Horgan's ability to inspire the creative energies of the cast, that many company members voiced discontent: If *Hair* were truly a communal endeavor as professed, should not the ensemble have shared in the profits?[22]

THEMES

Hair sought to reflect the tribal rituals of the hippies. Inspired by Marshal McLuhan's global village, its themes mirrored a group-tribal activity searching for a new and meaningful way of life. Exploring alternatives to the standards, goals, and morality of the older generation, *Hair* tackled some of the most controversial and explosive issues of the day. The two predominant issues were the Vietnam War and racial inequality. The completely revised Broadway version extended its thematic concerns, while commenting on a wide range of tangential, antiestablishment issues: poverty, pollution, religion, the military, and in particular, sexual freedom.

Hair broke the bawdy-language barrier for theater. Formerly forbidden words appeared in its dialogue. Tame by today's standards, the profane and obscene expressions both shocked and titillated the audiences. While the authors were very specific about not using *fuck* in any ad-libbing onstage, the word is repeated over and over again by Berger and Claude in a scene near the end of the second act, climaxing in, "Oh, fuckey fuckey, fuck, fuck." The topic of sexual freedom, which had been muted at the Public, was now highlighted with the addition of the song "Sodomy," the lyrics of which catalogued five human sexual practices using scientific terminology: sodomy, fellatio, cunnilingus, pederasty, and masturbation. But the show's most controversial (and commercial) issue was the nude scene during the Be-In, for *Hair* was the first show on Broadway to include total nudity of both men and women.[23]

While the nudity was responsible for a great deal of critical controversy, some thought it was less objectionable than others. Some expressed dismay that the formerly tame show now shocked by its meritricious display of the human body. Although the scene had been suggested in the original script, Papp vetoed it and Freedman thought it not germane. "I felt they wanted to get someone undressed just for the sake of getting them undressed. It was big at the time, getting undressed onstage, getting arrested by the cops. I thought it was exhibitionism. I wasn't opposed to nudity, but the intellectual idea behind it revolted me."[24]

In keeping with the authors' vision, O'Horgan saw the act as a symbolic act of freedom, honesty, and openness, a gentle defiance of another of society's taboos. People frequently took off their clothes at Be-Ins. It was part of the gesture of the times.[25] O'Horgan, who had used nudity before in his off-Broadway productions, observed that, "This was a different kind of nudity than had been on stage, quite different from *Oh! Calcutta!* and the nine million shows that followed and had to have a nude scene no matter what. The nudity was part of the freedom, part of the liberation."[26]

Barnes saw Castelli as the genie in the bottle. "Someone who was very important to all this was Louis Bertrand Castelli. It's very difficult to overestimate what Castelli did in terms of entrepreneurship,'' Barnes reflected. ''I'm not sure that the Love-In wasn't Castelli's idea, rather than O'Horgan's. I'm not sure, but certainly it was Castelli who gave it the green light.[27]

Barnes, who had known the impresario from his days at the Harkness and before that in Paris, remembers having a drink with him at the Sherry-Netherland about two weeks before the opening. Castelli announced that there was to be a nude Be-In. Barnes was utterly amazed. ''Although nudity had just about started on the New York stage, there had been one or two slight things, the idea of total frontal nudity was quite unusual.''[28] Barnes's initial reaction was that the show would be closed by the police. Castelli replied that he'd sent out a number of feelers, that he'd ''tested the climate,'' and ''presumably to his own satisfaction, he decided the police were unlikely.''[29]

Continuing on the possibility of being closed, Barnes asked, ''What happens if you are?'' Castelli paused, and then said, ''It'll be wonderful publicity, and it won't matter anyway.''[30]

THE PLOT

In all of its versions, *Hair*'s action revolves around three central characters: Claude, who gets drafted; a hippie high school dropout named Berger who will not go to war; and Sheila, an NYU college student who opposes America's involvement in Southeast Asia. The action centers on Claude's vacillation over the draft, which is pitted against the hardcore hippie attitude of Berger and the left-wing stance of Sheila. Berger, who remains true to the hippie ethos, is the counterculture ''hero'' of the piece. While there are some romantic entanglements, it is Claude's conflict that dominates the plot.

The important tribe members include: Hud, the black hippie; Woof, the seemingly-gay or pansexual hippie; Jeanie, the spiritual-mystical, pregnant hippie; and Crissy, the lost-soul hippie. Integral to the structure are Claude's parents, whose values contrast to those of the hippies. A sympathetic Mom and Dad in the Public Theater version attempted to bridge the generation gap. The burlesqued Broadway parents serve simply as objects of ridicule (as do authority figures in general). A strong "whiff of campy homosexuality" permeates their portrayals. Mom is played not by a middle-aged suburban-type female, but by three actors, one of them a young male in drag.[31]

THE STAGING

Time: the present. *Place:* New York City, mostly the East Village. *The set:* The bare stage, totally exposed, no wing masking. If possible, the entire proscenium arch is stripped of any curtain, thus exposing the fly area, the grid, etc. The stagehands, the stage managers, the actors, waiting for cues can be seen by the audience.[32]

Set designer Robin Wagner based his no-curtain design on the authors' ideas. The fly area and wings were exposed to the full view of the audience. "As far as the scenery, the lighting, the production, and all the rest of it was concerned," he remarked, "basically what we were doing was allowing the audience to be part of it. Showing everything. Letting it all hang out, as it were."[33] There was no masking. The brick walls, the radiator pipes, the stage ropes, the light-pipes, and all the lights were exposed Rado suggested a raked stage for greater immediacy—unusual for a musical that included choreography. Wagner incorporated it into the design. A tower of abstract scaffolding upstage at the rear of the rake merged an authentic American Indian totem pole and a modern sculptured Crucifix-Tree, the two set pieces indicated in the stage directions. The tribe climbed and performed various gymnastics upon the scaffolding, which was decorated with hippie artifacts and other absurd convention icons, *objets trouvee* gathered by cast and crew from the streets of New York. The treasure trove included a rubber tire, a jukebox, a large electric eyeball, the head of Jesus, a lifesize papier maché bus driver behind a steering wheel, a Coca-Cola sign, and a neon marquee of the Waverly movie theater of Greenwich Village.

Upstage to the right of the scaffolding was a Plexiglas and steel structure about ten feet high, which served as a platform for the "Supremes" number. The proscenium arch was outlined with scaffolding also suitable for climbing. On the rear upstage wall hung a large scenic flat of the American flag which was lit from within. The entire set was painted in shades of gray, and street graffiti was stenciled onto the raked stage, which had spotlights built into it, as well as a trapdoor for Jeanie's entrances.

The Biltmore had only two-thirds of the lighting capacity available to the average Broadway musical. This served as no deterrent to innovative lighting designer Jules Fisher. A relatively limited palette of five colors coming from four directions allowed for many permutations. "I could have the whole stage in any one color from any one direction or mix those. It was just the combination of those," Fisher stated, "that seemed so varied."[34] Color, shade, and intensity were based on the tempo and temper of the music and the emotions that occurred within the framework of the script.[35] The LSD stroboscopic sequence was a psychedelic light show, timed to over 108 lighting cures. Prior to computerized boards, it required three technicians frantically working the levers with their hands, elbows, knees, and even feet.[36] The auditorium was lit with glaring spots, as requested by O'Horgan, and with the sculptural design of Hindu and Indian patterns, suggested by Wagner. These lighting schemes were repeated throughout the play.[37]

Adding to the theatricality, the band was placed onstage in a hollowed out truck.[38] Heavily amplified, and now under the musical direction of the composer, the musical ensemble was enlarged from five to nine. "It was a bigger theatre, we had to make more noise,"[39] says MacDermot. To the electric keyboard, guitars, and percussion used at the Public Theater, a brass and woodwind section was added.

With eight large loudspeakers and an emphasis on amplification, the decibel level was considerably above the norm for Broadway audiences. Chest mikes seemed to be the answer to the problem of lyrics being drowned out by instrumental din, but they proved dysfunctional during frenetic dance movements. In the end, O'Horgan elected to go with standard hand mikes, cords fully exposed to the audience.[40]

Speaking about the show's choreography, O'Horgan made no excuses about his role: "Basically, I did all the dance movements."[41] Nevertheless, the job of instructing *Hair*'s cast in the intricacies of dance fell to Julie Arenal. Like Sokolow before her, Arenal faced a cast with little or no dance experience, and while *Hair* lacked full-scale dance numbers, it had its performers in a perpetual state of motion. Determined to avoid the artificiality of the off-Broadway choreography, Arenal encouraged the troupe to remain "loose" and "natural," relying on dance movements that were individualized, organic and natural.[42] Interviewed by *Dance Magazine*'s Ronald Gold, Arenal acknowledged that O'Horgan's assault on the fourth wall was her essential frame of reference, "the kids in the aisles and up on ladders," and that she agreed the show would have no predetermined dance movements, "every number should have a different physical conception. . . . All movements evolving from the situation, changing shapes and levels."[43] As with dialogue, the cast was encouraged to develop the details of their movements in rehearsals, and there was some freedom of expression even after the piece was set. For example, there might be four bars of music that allowed for vertical or horizontal expression, wherein the dancers were allowed individual forms of interpretation.

The costumes by Nancy Potts, which were realistic yet

highly theatrical in color, texture, and inventiveness, were based directly on hippie "street" clothes, which she observed were getting "wilder and wilder."[44] An elaboration on the hippie jeans, feathers, and beads, her costumes included bell-bottomed jeans with Ukrainian-embroidered strips sewn along the seams, ripped clothes, tie-dyed T-shirts, military jackets, mixed military uniforms, a red-white-and-blue fringed coat, and a huge dark blue velvet cape for Berger to wear as George Washington on his horse in the Valley Forge part of the trip sequence. The most innovative and amusing of her designs was the Supremes costume, one large (size 60), fucshia-colored, sequined tube dress made of stretch material, which enclosed a trio of black girls and appeared to be three floor-length gowns. On cue the trio would step apart, revealing the dress to be only one. Melba Moore, who played Diana Ross, one of the Supremes, vividly recalls the moment as a personal highlight. When the audiences realized it was one dress, "they cracked up."[45]

HAIR'S ORGANIC STRUCTURE

Critical reaction to the Papp production had been positive, but without an unqualified endorsement. Although the reviewers had mixed feelings for *Hair*, they had only unmixed feelings for the vitality of the piece under Freedman's brilliant direction, its score, and its contemporary relevance. Somewhat disarmed by the engaging spirits of the youngsters, many critics recognized that the show was "potentially terrific," implying that it somehow failed to meet its full "potential." Most notably, *Hair* was faulted for its book, or more specifically, lack of book.[46] "Still the critics knew that something important had happened. A fresh new wind had literally blown away the old concepts of musicals."[47]

Aware of the need for revision, Ragni, Rado, and Mac-Dermot had begun writing new materials while still at the

Public. However, with O'Horgan as the inspirational gadfly, *Hair* continued to be transformed in the process of the rehearsal period.

But the changes did not stop there. In her autobiographical book, *Letting Down My Hair*, cast member Lorrie Davis contended that *Hair* was virtually a different show every night, owing to the improvisations. Responding to whether *Hair* was a different show every night, O'Horgan answered, "Well, no theatre is, and that's what's good about theatre. And this was the extreme, of course. I'd go away and do another show, come back, and *Hair* would be like another show. It was a living organism, more than any other piece I've ever been involved in."[48]

The element of play was very much a part of the performance. "We changed the lines all the time," said Davis. "People (cast) were waiting to see what we would do next. And it was funny, and it worked."[49]

According to O'Horgan, one of the aspects of the show was to keep it open. The cast would come up with things during the comic moments, and if they worked, they would be incorporated into the show. For the most part changes had to do with current events. If the show was in Chicago, "you did that which was applicable to Chicago, since the cast all came from Chicago. The cast came from the city it was being performed in. So there was a kind of investment of the territory in it, which was another kind of strength of the piece."[50] In 1971, O'Horgan directed *Lenny*, based on the Lenny Bruce story. "Everybody thought Lenny did a lot of improvisation. He might do as much as 10 percent an evening, but there was a structure that he worked from."[51] The same applied to *Hair*. To keep a sense of spontaneity, improvisation was encouraged within the framework and timing of the piece.

From this perspective, *Hair* was a different show every night. Improvisation occurred within the comic moments. Rehearsals continued to produce creative nuances, and the authors continued to explore the possibilities of their script.

Stagings in locations around the globe were adapted to local allusions. And the ad-libbing never ceased. Thus, the reader may recall certain variations on the "Biltmore reconstruction" or when reading the published Tams Witmark script. What's really wrong with most published scripts, O'Horgan explained, is that they suffer from author's revenge. No director cuts without the author's consent and participation. But when the script is published, all the cuts are put back into the script. "Everything gets published, which is OK. This allows other directors to pick and choose, make cuts. But most people don't realize this, and when they try to put a show on, as a consequence, it becomes an extraordinary piece of unfocused stuff, which is what we frequently see in revivals."[52]

OPENING NIGHT AT THE BILTMORE

The following is a reconstruction of the *Hair* that audiences saw at the Biltmore on opening night, April 29, 1968. The information is based on frequent dialogues with the authors. All subsequent productions were governed by the Broadway script, which is considered the "authentic" version of *Hair*. The scenes overlap and merge, one scene dissolving into another in a cinematic structure.

The Vamp

There is no curtain. The cast is scattered throughout the theater in the orchestra, in the balconies, on the scaffolding and the stage. Jim Rado sits crossed-legged in Indian style, stage center, staring vacantly into a small fire before him. On cue, the tribe members freeze, and then proceed in slow motion to the stage. Claude is joined by Sheila (Lynn Kellogg) and Berger (Gerome Ragni), who cut a strand of

Claude's hair, ceremoniously offering it to the fire, in an act
that symbolically foreshadows his sacrifice to the establishment. The show's concept is established from the moment the
audience enters the theater. The tribe prepares for the
ceremony, the ritual, the play: *Hair*. They are about to
demonstrate their way of life. In presenting their story, they
hope to gain greater understanding and a saner, peace-full,
love-full world. They attempt to "turn on" the audience.

"Aquarius" (The Tribe Introduce Themselves)

The tribe has gathered. Without an overture, Ron (Ronnie
Dyson) launches into the astrologically predicting "Aquarius." He mystically calls forth visions of a new age and a
flowering of harmony and understanding.

Donna (Berger Introduces Himself)

Medusan-haired, Berger strips down to his Native American loincloth, introduces himself. He casually wanders into
the audience, and ends his monologue sitting in the lap of a
female audience member in the third row, asking for a handout to "keep his chromosomes dancing." "I know what
you're thinking," he says. "Isn't he a cute one. What is it, a
boy or a girl?" He sings a frantically paced rock number
about a sixteen-year old virgin (the eponymous Donna)
whom he lost in Tompkins Square Park and has been searching for in San Francisco. The peripatetic high school student
tells the audience that he's seen most of the world. He's
conversed with yogis in India, smoked pot in South America.
Still scantily clad, he climbs to a box above the proscenium
arch. Continuing in song, he mounts a rope, swings out over
the heads of the audience and then back to the stage. The
song establishes his frenetic and liberated personality; his

predisposition to noncompliant behavior. He breaks societal rules. He breaks fourth wall reality.

"Hashish" (The Tribe Introduce Drugs)

The tribe scatters into small groupings on the stage, and Berger sings "Hashish." The lyrics of the song inventory the tribe's answer to mind-altering substances and raised levels of consciousness. Hashish, cocaine, heroin, opium, LSD, and morning glory seeds, and other hallucinogens common to the earliest of cultures, where they were used in tribal spiritual tradition, are rhapsodized.

"Sodomy" (Introduces Woof)

Drugs are not the only thing that the tribe has on its collective mind. They assume mock religious posturings, with two members of the company posing as Madonna and Infanta. Woof (Steve Curry) a pansexual love child with a yearning for Mick Jagger, sings "Sodomy," a mock-solemn tribute to a few special examples of profane love. The lyrics sing in glowing terms of sodomy, fellatio, cunnilingus, and pederasty as if they were sacraments. The Catholic-raised Woof asks why the words sound so perverse. Not a sign of hubris, his question seems to involve some soul-searching. One wonders if the song is his confessional or a referendum opposed to such societal taboos. Although he doesn't practice what he sings, he wonders about certain improprieties as he confesses that masturbation can be "fun."

Colored Spade (Introduces Hud)

Hanging upside down from a pole, Hud (Lamont Washington), who is black, is carried to the stage by two white hippies. Dressed like a medicine man, he sings a tune of racial prejudice that includes a string of derogatory epithets that have been hurled at blacks. The litany includes *jungle-bunny*, *jigaboo*, *pickaninny*, *cotton-picker*, as well as a new appelation: *President of the United States of Love.*

Manchester (Introduces Claude)

As Hud sings about his experiences in "Colored Spade," Claude stands in a washtub. He wears a British flag for a loincloth. Three black girls tar and feather his white body. Using a watering can as a shower, the girls then wash the mud and feathers from his body in a symbolic exorcism of racial pejoratives. But they can't wash away the fact that Claude comes from "dirty, slummy, mucky, polluted," Flushing, Queens. Holding a hand mike, Claude sings wistfully about himself in "Manchester, England." Having mastered the British affectations of language, he fantasizes that he comes from Manchester, mistaking it perhaps as the home of the Beatles.

"Ain't Got No" (Poverty)

Hud, Woof, and Dionne (Melba Moore) give the audience a lesson in the microeconomics of the hippie lifestyle in the song "Ain't Got No." They sing a series of "ain't got no's" followed by the words *home*, *shoes*, *money*, *class*, *scarf*, *gloves*, *bed*, *pot*, *faith* to which the tribe chimes in antiphonal responses: *so*, *poor*, *honey*, *common*, *cold*, *beat*, *busted*, *Catholic*. Their poverty is self-imposed, but they do hope that Dad will continue to send money.

"I Believe in Love" (Introduces Jeanie)

The shopping list of primarily material have-nots is followed by Sheila's song "I Believe in Love." Appearing on stage as if on horseback, she extols the true meaning of existence and love—spiritual, communal, and carnal. The tune reveals her character. Sheila is a love-guided "flower child," committed to the left. She leads the tribe in a chant. "What do we want?" "Peace!" "When do we want it?" "Now!"

"Air" (Jeanie Pops Up and Introduces Herself)

Claude, Berger, Woof, and Hud gasp for air, as Jeanie emerges from a "manhole" trapdoor built into the stage. She offers a paean to pollution, welcoming sulfur dioxide, saying hello to carbon monoxide. Her tune ends in a fit of coughing, during which she urges the establishment audience to breath deeply.

"Initials" (Breakdown in Human Relationships/Language)

The tribe pokes fun at the illiterate sloganizing of language. Simulating a classroom experience, they sing the imaginative and playful parody "Initials." LBJ somehow manages to get on the IRT. The lyrics suggest an awareness of the general decay of language, and the audience senses that hippies refuse to be reduced to a depersonalized string of letters.

Mom and Dad Sequence (Establishment Makes an Entry)

In an embellishment of the original script, Claude's parents in triplicate step to the stage from the audience where they have been seated. The aggressive Moms are played by two females and one male, the ineffective Dads by two males and one female, thus heightening their stereotypic presentations.

They chastise Claude because of his "disgusting" hippie garb, and take particular delight in presenting him with his draft notice, which arrived that morning.

"I Got Life" (Claude's Dialogue with the Older Generation)

Mom urges Claude to change his trousers and take off the beads. He reminds Mom that it's 1968, not 1948. "What have you got, 1968," she responds, "that makes you do damn superior and gives me such a headache?" Claude answers in "I Got Life," a song that celebrates his body. He's got his hair, his head, his brains, his ears, his tits, and his ass, down to his toes. He's got good times and bad times just like his parents. His ways seem crazy, but he's a human being, too.

"Going Down" (Bad Berger Gets Expelled)

Three tribe members impersonate authoritarian school principals replete with Hitlerian moustaches. Declaring World War III, they expel Berger for violating the PS 183 Personal Appearance Code for refusing to cut his long locks. Elated, Berger makes a dramatic leap from the scaffolding tower into the arms of his trusted friends. He sings "Going Down," perceiving his situation analogous to Lucifer's banishment to Hell. He's been expelled from high school Heaven.

"*Hair*"

However, it is Claude, not Berger, who is in real trouble. Taking center stage, he informs the tribe that he has passed his induction physical and is about to be drafted. A Man and a Woman appear from the audience, interrupting the group's emotional response to Claude's announcement. They go up onto the stage. The man carries a camera, pencil, and notebook, somewhat similar to a tourist/reporter. He timidly asks the hippies who their heroes are. Woof displays a poster: Jesus was a Catholic. The tribe cite comic book characters: Wonder Woman, Prince Valiant, and Orphan Annie.

"My Conviction"

The Woman who has emerged from the audience asks why the hippies wear their hair so long. Her curiosity seques into the title song. Led by Berger and Claude, the tribe sings that they really don't know why, but it is still a God-given cause for celebration. In "My Conviction," the tourist lady offers an anthropological justification regarding the emergence of the male from his drab camouflage. Her attempts at rationalization are met with a rousing, "Fuck you, Margaret Meade," which punctuates the scene. But as a coda to the ending, she slaps down a wild card, throws open her fur coat, and reveals that she is a man in drag.

"Easy to Be Hard"

Sheila enters center stage. For Berger, with whom she is enamored, she brings back a yellow satin shirt from her protest in D.C. In giving the gift to Berger, she interrupts his rap session with the boys. He accuses her of nagging jealousy. His volatile temper flairs, and he tears the gift to bits. Sheila sings "Easy to Be Hard," wondering how people can be so heartless. Jeanie appears once more from her trapdoor manhole, rendering a short dissertation on romantic entanglements. She loves Claude, but Claude loves Sheila and Berger. Sheila loves Berger, but Berger is "hung up everywhere." And, of course, Hud loves Mick Jagger.

"Don't Put It Down"

Originally entitled, "Red, Blue, and White," this song opened the downtown show and was sung by Claude's parents. On Broadway, Berger, Woof, and Ron harmonize a love song to the American flag in the retitled "Don't Put It Down." Tripping on its colors, the red, blue, white, and yellow fringe, they proclaim that it's the best flag around. While the trio holds the flag in preparation for folding, a stoned Woof falls into it like it is a hammock, saying, "I'm falling through a hole in the flag." As they sing, they fold the flag according to prescribed military regulations, with something of a redneck patriotic fervor.

"Frank Mills" (Crissy's Solo)

As the flag scene concludes, the tribe rushes from the wings to the stage and into the audience. They distribute flyers, inviting the audience to the Be-In. The tribe disappears offstage to change into more colorful Be-In costumes. Waiflike Crissy (Shelley Plimpton), alone, downstage right, sings the quiet ballad "Frank Mills." With a gentle naivete, she describes the boy she met in front of the Waverly movie house, and has not seen since. She's lost his address, but she knows he lives in Brooklyn. He wears his hair tied back in a bow and has gold chains on his leather jacket. Appealing to the audience, she asks that should they see him, to relay the message that she and her girlfriend Angela are looking for him. (Crissy's song was one of the highlights of the show.)

"Be-In" and "Where Do I Go"

The sound of bells is heard from offstage, from the back of the theater, and from the aisles. The tribe enters from all directions with ankle, wrist, and hand bells, carrying candles and incense. The audience is surrounded with insistent rhythms that build as the tribe in their colorful costumes, beads, feathers, and face paint, frolic to the strains of "Hare Krishna." The Be-In has begun. A small tripod holding a can of fire is set up, around which the tribe huddles in blankets. One by one, the young males burn their draft cards. Sheila offers a daffodil in exchange. Claude is last. He approches the fire, has second thoughts and retrieves his card from the flames. He probes the meaning of life and death in "Where Do I Go." Should he follow the river, follow the wind? The tribe crawls under a scrim stretched across the entire stage floor as they answer, suggesting in song that he follow the innocent children and their smiles. The music fades. Moments later the tribe comes from openings in the scrim into the audience's view. They stand naked and motionless, their bodies bathed in Fisher's light projection of floral patterns. They chant of beads, flowers, freedom, and happiness. A police siren is heard, and a rotating red police car light beams across the audience. The hippies pick up their clothes and run from the darkened stage. The houselights come up, and two policemen appear in the orchestra aisle, announcing that the audience is "under arrest for watching this lewd and obscene show." (So realistic was the interpretation of this scene, so taken in was the audience by the illusion, in the ultimate of Brechtian techniques, that the actors were compelled to reveal their joke, announcing, "It's only intermission.")

"Electric Blues"

Act II begins as Hud walks onto a dimly lit stage carrying an antique windup Victrola. Crissy puts on a recording, and they listen to Kate Smith's rendition of "The White Cliffs of Dover." The old-fashioned melody merges into the full rock sound of "Electric Blues." Four cast members in mirrored costumes sing and dance wildly during an elaborate psychedelic light show. Their ode to the age of electricity proclaims old tunes are definitely not *au courant.*

As the dancing ends, Claude revs up the audience in another unanticipated moment. Dressed in a gorilla suit and growling at the audience, he rides a motorcycle from the back of the orchestra, down the center aisle, and up onto center stage. (Joe Butler, who took over the role says he "scared the Bejesus out of some of the audience members, who would really start moving out of the way.") Claude takes off his gorilla head, revealing his identity. He tells the audience that he has once again visited the induction center on Whitehall Street. In the background, Berger and cast reenact a mock version of the scene at the draft board. In an act of suicidal resignation, Claude gives away his prized possession, a poster of Mick Jagger, to Woof.

"Black Boys"/"White Boys" (Motown Makes It to Broadway)

Three white girls (Diane Keaton, Suzannah Norstrand, and Linda Compton) appear on stage and sing "Black Boys" to Hud, expressing their sexual attraction to chocolate-flavored treats. They are intensely upstaged by the overpowering appearances and voices of three black girls (Melba Moore, Lorrie Davis, and Emmaretta Marks). Positioned on a ten-foot Plexiglas platform that glides toward the audience, the trio, attired in bouffant wigs and sexy-cheap sequined gowns, belt out a Supremes impersonation of "White Boys," which they dedicate to Claude. The hilarious bit takes on added theatricality when the trio step apart and their seemingly three dresses are in fact one.

"Walking in Space" (The Tribe Trips)

The band has stopped playing. The tribe speaks in low voices. Hud switches off the lights. For a moment the stage is in darkness, but candles are lit. Berger, wearing dark glasses, passes out sticks of marijuana to the tribe. The stage lights up as the tribe lights up. There is no talking and no music—only the sound of inhaling. To the rocking rhythm of a snare drum and brush, the tribe begins a freeform homage linking psychedelic drugs with universal consciousness and the satellites orbiting the globe. They sing about their bodies walking in space, their souls in orbit, and about being face-to-face with God. The lights dim with just a follow-spot on Claude. Before leaving for the killing fields, he stays the midnight bell, takes LSD, and has his last gaudy night. Then follows a hallucinogenic synopsis of American history enacted on stage representing Claude's trip.

Berger, impersonating George Washington, powdered wig askew, wearing a huge, dark-blue, flowing velvet cape, rides on his horse through Valley Forge. He carries a battleworn American flag and leads a bedraggled army of about half a dozen tribe members (all female), whom he summarily orders to retreat. He flees as four Indians in loincloths with tomahawks and warpaint massacre his troops. General Grant in a Confederate uniform appears and revives the army, which turns out to be an anachronistic mix made up of Abraham Lincoln, John Wilkes Booth, Calvin Coolidge, Clark Gable, Scarlett O'Hara, Teddy Roosevelt, and General Custer. Lincoln, who is played by Lorrie Davis, is the most elaborately costumed of the cross-dressed troupe, attired in a finely brocaded, black velvet jacket; red, white, and blue stockings; and a contrasting "stoved-in" hat. The curious assembly dances a minuet. They are attacked from behind by three African witch doctors in feathers. Chief witch doctor Hud berates Lincoln on America's racial inequality, commenting that Vietnam is a prime example of racial exploitation: the white man has sent the black man to fight the yellow man to defend a country stolen from the red man. Davis as Lincoln responds in a jived version of the Gettysburg Address, while a white girl shines Lincoln's shoes with her long blonde hair. The witch doctors are transformed into a Black Power group. They sing a satirical "Happy Birthday Abie Baby," after which they shoot Lincoln, who falls dead but rises to inveigh, "Shit, I ain't dying for no white man."

Claude's trip continues as four Buddhist monks in traditional robes appear onstage. In a page taken from the newspapers of the day, one of the monks pours gasoline on himself, sets himself on fire, and dies in an agonizing protest against the Vietnam War. In rapid-fire succession, three Catholic nuns, reciting the rosary, kill the remaining Buddhists; three astronauts enter and kill the nuns with ray guns; three Chinese with machine guns kill the astronauts; four American Indians tomahawk the Chinese; and they are killed by Green Berets wielding machine guns. The killing orgy seems to end when the Green Berets turn their weapons on themselves. The bodies lie in a heap, "ripped open by metal explosion." A strobe light flashes on, and the killing scene goes into reverse. All the bodies come back to life, exit backward, and reenter at an accelerated pace, going through the exact same ritual, this time to the cacophony of machine guns and other fierce sounds of war. Sound and strobe lights cease, and the stage lights are brought up, revealing bodies once again in a motionless heap.

There is a momentary relief of silence. A mournful bugle is heard from the wings, as a drill sergeant calls the roll. Two parents carry onstage a man's suit of clothing on a hanger, which symbolically represents their son. They speak to their son, bidding him goodbye. "Write me a letter," says Mom. "You don't know how proud I am," says Dad. A childlike nursery tune is heard in the distance. In slow motion, one by one the bodies rise. Transformed into small children, they begin playing children's games that quickly degenerate into simulated combat. The company sings "Three-Five-Zero-Zero," which begins as a whisper and mounts into an anguished crescendo that expresses the devastating futility of war. Two members of the group (Ronnie Dyson and Walter

Harris) have been observing the war games from the central scaffolding. They descend and sing "What a Piece of Work Is Man." Taking their inspiration from a passage in Shakespeare's *Hamlet*, the lyrics contrast the inherent nobility of human nature with the "pestilent congregation of vapors" present in human conflict, like the napalm vapors of Vietnam. The two singers walk among the dead, and then fall among them.

The lights change, and the bodies come to a sitting position. They link hands and sing about their mystical revelation— "our eyes are open." The lights come down. A spot on Claude, as at the beginning of the war sequence, indicates that his trip is over. Claude wishes for redemptive powers of holy white snow. He doesn't want to go into the army in the morning. He wishes he were invisible, so he could do anything, go anywhere, be free, and be happy.

"Good Morning Starshine" (Sheila Offers an Optimistic View)

It is late at night on the street, time for everyone to part and go home. Sheila appears at center stage. Radiating an emotional glow of universal love, she sings "Good Morning Starshine" up to the heavens. The lyrics of the song offer a comforting correspondence between human beings and the unknown life in the stars. The tribe joins in a light-hearted dance.

"The Bed" (The Last Fling)

Crissy is carried from the audience on a mattress which the tribe has found on the street. They exuberantly dance and sing in a last fling of revelry about the things that can be done in bed. They include eating crackers and cheese, but never sinning in bed. The song ends. The mood changes, and the tribe takes their leave of Claude. Each expresses an individual fond farewell to the musical accompaniment of "Aquarius." The company disappears into the wings. At the margin of the stage, an army sergeant, rifle at parade rest, awaits his new inductee. Claude attempts to retreat. A shot rings out, and another. He doubles over and disappears into the upstage shadows.

The sound of a conch shell emanates from the rear of the orchestra. The tribe returns from all directions, banging homemade rhythm instruments and garbage can lids, and blowing whistles. Woof drags a large metal washtub onto the stage. With heavy drumming sticks, Berger joins Hud, beating a frantic rhythm. The scene is in front of the Army Induction Center on Whitehall Street. The boisterous activity builds to a crescendo—"Hell no, we won't go." Sheila and Berger search for Claude. The tribe calls out his name. Suddenly Claude appears dressed in an army uniform, his hair neatly shorn. "I'm right here," he answers. "Like it or not, they got me." But his voice is not heard, and he is not seen by his friends. He has become invisible. The tribe freezes, as time seemingly stands still.

"The Flesh Failures" and "Let the Sun Shine In" (Claude Dies, but the Tribe Lives on)

Standing at rigid attention upstage center, Claude begins the opening lines of "The Flesh Failures." He walks directly downstage and sings the refrain of "Manchester, England." A trio sings the counterpoint "Eyes Look Your Last." Claude backs up, as the tribe advances and surrounds him. They feel his presence and stretch out their hands to touch what they cannot see in a stage picture that covers Claude's image. He disappears from audience view. Sheila and Dionne take up the lead of "The Flesh Failures" ("Let the Sun Shine In"). The tribe moves downstage to the front lip of the stage, entreating the audience to join in song. There is a final explosion of movement, waving, dancing, holding hands; and then the tribe parts center stage, walking off into opposite wings, still singing. Claude is seen lying lifeless on a black grave at the center of the stage. Berger, who has remained behind, dances furiously in a circular motion. He goes upstage of Claude's body, falls to one knee, and thrusts his two white drumming sticks above his friend's head in the image of a cross. The lights dim as we hear the final refrain of "Let the Sun Shine In." The lights go black, and all the audience sees is the Day-glo cross shining through the darkness.

The ending left many audience members in a somewhat trancelike state. Breaking the momentary spell, they rose to give the cast a standing ovation, calling them back onstage for the encore of the title song "Hair." And performer and spectator became one, as audience members jumped to the aisles and were pulled to the stage to dance in a joyous act of the celebration of life.

HAIR'S CONTROVERSIAL ISSUES

Antiestablishment in form and content, *Hair* created a revolution and a critical maelstrom about a number of issues from diverse quarters. This section considers the various controversies over form, music, and other iconoclastic contrasts in values, and attempts to offer an understanding as to their intent.

Form

O'Horgan's productions are "colorful, unabashedly frenetic and joyful, but they also tend to obscure story and idea."[53] And his tendency to subordinate script to directorial manner caused much critical consternation. Clive Barnes reported that the authors had done a "very brave thing in throwing out the book entirely." He said the revised book is "about as identifiable as the Manhattan telephone directory."[54] Composer-director Lehman Engel summarily attacked the current "rock nontheater musicals" as plotless, characterless, directionless theater happenings, ranking *Hair* the most successful of the "new nonplot shows," even with its characters that are "pretty much alike and indistinguishable, one from another."[55]

In its staging, some critics noted a reversion to the early revues, *The Black Crook* and those of the Kiralfys. In terms of form, still others, as Taubman of the *Times*, thought the story line so attenuated that it should be "merciful to label the piece a revue." But Gottfried correctly maintained that "*Hair* was not a revue, because while *Hair*'s songs may not have advanced the narrative line, they were unmistakably an extension of the characters' emotions within a specific dramatic situation, each song an "essay on the character's feelings."[56]

Rado believed that he contributed to an imbroglio over nomenclature. In an early interview with Dan Sullivan at the Public Theater, he remarked that *Hair* was a nonbook musical, based on the fact that the show had twice as many songs as the standard Broadway musical.[57] In concert with Ragni, and sounding much like Shakespeare's Polonius, Rado averred that "*Hair* on its most basic structural level was a musical comedy, or a musical comedy-tragedy, or just a plain musical, in that it was composed of both songs and scenes."[58] Beyond this, the authors were unable to arrive at a more exacting categorization for their creation, describing it as a "hybrid of the revue form and the integrated book form, an advancement of the integrated form, something so seamless and unpredictable that it defied intellectual analysis."[59]

While O'Horgan likened the form to that of the comic

opera *The Magic Flute*—a little bit of dialogue and a lot of music—he allowed that *Hair* did lack a "structural plot like you see in a Neil Simon play," but noted that "the same can be said of Ibsen's *Peer Gynt*, so that *Hair* is a nonplot piece only in the narrowest sense."[60] Given time for analytical reflection Harriet and Irving Deer observed in 1978, that the genius of *Hair* in line with *Singin' in the Rain* and *A Chorus Line* "lies in style and performance rather than plot and character conventions."[61]

Theatrically conceived during the rehearsal-workshop period, the Broadway show relied heavily on production elements tied to the theme of the hippie lifestyle, organically blending text, song, and dance, adhering to the definition of the concept musical. The authors scripted much of the Broadway show from the workshop creativity, which presented the hippie generation in rebellion. Working closely with O'Horgan, they assembled the show into a cinematic script arrangement wherein sequences intertwined, overlapped, and flashed backward and forward. The fact that *Hair* was Broadway's first fully realized concept musical seemed to have escaped critical attention.

In his book *Broadway Musicals*, Martin Gottfried coined the term "concept musical." In a recent interview, he offered a firsthand definition: "A book musical is called a book musical because it is based on a script. A concept musical is based on the production, what Hal Prince would call an 'umbrella metaphor.' It starts out with some stage notion, it's theatrical. Whereas the book musical is written, the playwright writes it, and the director just stages it, puts actors into those roles, the concept musical is created in rehearsal."[62]

Jerome Robbins's *West Side Story* (1957), and *Fiddler on the Roof* (1964) are considered the beginnings of the concept musical, followed by Harold Prince's *Cabaret* (1966), which is half conventional book musical, half concept musical. *West Side Story* put the streets of New York onstage; *Fiddler*, the shtetl; and *Cabaret*, the Kit Kat Club. As there seemed little question that *Hair* extended the very same production approach in its attempts to put the hippie lifestyle onstage, the author asked Gottfried directly, if *Hair* was not a concept musical. "Not the Freedman production," he replied. "That was a conventional book show. The O'Horgan production, yes."

"They probably did learn a great deal in the process— being that they were dopey actors. They probably began stumbling their way along, and in the process they learned from O'Horgan, who was really at his peak then. And they saw the thing changing in production."[63] Gottfried further allowed that O'Horgan was very much involved in the look of it, as opposed to the script or dialogue, as was Julie Arenal, the choreographer, and less and less emphasis was placed on the dialogue.[64]

Then, why wasn't *Hair* recognized as the first fully realized concept musical? Gottfried replied because, like everybody else, "I frankly didn't take it seriously."[65]

> Broadway was dead set against it. *Hair* was done by out-siders. Remember Broadway is a very small place. It's really very inbred. If you weren't a David Merrick, an Alex Cohen, or a Hal Prince, you didn't belong to the family. You were an outsider. *Hair* was brought in by outsiders. It wasn't written by Jerry Herman or Charles Strouse, or Cy Coleman, and worst of all, it had this "f---ing" music that everybody hated. Everybody wanted it to be *Guys and Dolls* forever. They just weren't paying any attention to what was on the radio. The audiences were getting older, and older, and older, and *Hair* had nothing to do with their music. And when *Hair* came in on Broadway, the Broadway people were flabbergasted, confused, and angry, because they didn't know what this thing was or how it could be a success. It failed every one of their standards. It wasn't their kind of stuff, and they finally wrote it off as just a freak.[66]

The Score

Hair was billed as a rock musical, but was its music "authentic" rock? A controversy over whether *Hair* was a sincere attempt to reflect the hippie counterculture or merely a blatant commercialization became the focus of a debate about the musical's genre. Was it "rock" or was it "pop"? In an article entitled "Music and the Mass Culture Debate," Graham Vulliamy suggested that rock music was not commercial, as was the homogeneous, mass-oriented, standardized "pop," which deprived its artists control over creativity.[67] While some critics seized upon the commerciality of the score, thus rejecting *Hair*'s music as "authentic" rock, others lauded "its tenuous position between the hip and the commercial, between the popular and the sophisticated, between artifice and nature,"[68] interpreting it as an attempt to bridge another generational gap.

Asked if the score was "authentic" rock, MacDermot was quick to reply that strictly defined rhythm does not lend itself to drama. In writing a show that tells a story and has characters: "You have to write a lot of different kinds of tunes. Most rock composers write one kind, because they know that's what will sell. But you're not selling tunes in a show. You're contributing to the whole show. And that means variety. Every character has to have his own type of song."[69]

The score is not pure rock, but a confluence of jazz, blues, soul, country and western, raga, and rock. Commenting on the syncretic nature of the score, one critic noted that the members of the cast sang "all kinds of songs in many different styles and idioms, some with a strong rock beat, some primitive and formless, some with swinging and lusty emotions, and some with a good deal of tender feeling to them."[70] Gottfried called it "middle-range rock."[71] The music critic for the *Times* similarly wrote that MacDermot was able to "reach out and find considerable variety on the outskirts of his rock-bound core."[72] But the theater establishment wrote it off, because it "lumped together everything that the older generation associates with rock music: hippies, drug references, sex equals love, frug dancing, and light shows."[73]

"They just didn't like the music," Barnes recalled. "And of course, *Hair* was not really a rock musical. It was intended for the tourists, for the parents. And the scariest thing was that it ended up becoming very much a part of its time. Some of the tunes. "The Dawning of the Age of Aquarius," actually became imbedded very much in the *zeitgeist* of the period. It was taken seriously by people who perhaps one would never have expected. This was very interesting, I felt."[74]

With the advent of Elvis Presley (1956), and a little bit later the Beatles and the Rolling Stones, the whole fabric of popular music had changed, almost overnight, Barnes reflected. "Almost overnight, the music that was top of the charts— that was genuinely popular—no longer reflected Broadway music, Hollywood music. It was a new musical world, and even today, Broadway hasn't quite come to terms with this."[75]

In terms of *Hair*'s rock score, MacDermot affirmed, "Well about the only thing you can say is that the band was a rock band, two guitars, drums, a bass, and a keyboard. That's a standard rock band. But all the tunes, you couldn't categorize them that way, because every tune was different."[76] O'Horgan confirmed that the sound was rock:

> Rock is a very broad term. Not everything is hard acid rock. There are rock ballads. There are power ballads. It's almost impossible to make a musical all out of one kind of concept. I mean, if you go to any Mozart opera, you'll find the presence of a number of different styles. There are parody arias, there are romantic arias. . . . You just can't make an evening out of one kind of idea. The basic fix of the music in *Hair* is all from a rock standpoint. And there are as many aspects to rock as there are rock composers. And I do think that Galt is basically that kind of composer.[77]

Did It Belong on Broadway?

Hair was not the first musical to be transferred to Broadway. *The Golden Apple* and *Once upon a Mattress* had set precedent. However, *Hair* was the first rock musical to be moved from off-Broadway, albeit through the back door of political connections to the Great White Way. Among the composers, lyricists, book writers, and producers who were accustomed to exercising hegemony over what goes on uptown, reaction to *Hair* followed the conventional crisis sequence of denial, anger, and depression, but never reached acceptance. Richard Rodgers, Burt Bacharach, and Leonard Bernstein all attended Biltmore performances of *Hair*, each venting anger at its iconoclastic presence and expressing pessimism about the outlook for the American musical theater. David Merrick, who had turned the show down and a year and a half before, commented, "I don't know what the hell this is. I don't know why people like it."[78]

The confusion *Hair* engendered among Broadway's potentates was understandable. The show was the handiwork of off-off-Broadway primitives, as far as they were concerned, these "two dopey actors," and it had this terrible music. The real caper, however, was that *Hair* not only violated all of the standards that the Broadway nabobs held dear, but made them somewhat queasy in criticizing it, because one of the absolute rules on Broadway is that you "don't argue with a hit, and *Hair* was a huge hit."[79]

For a segment of the New York theater critic corps, *Hair*'s success was their Waterloo. These reviewers had used the strongest language that their publications would allow to try to persuade readers to avoid the Biltmore like plague. John Chapman of the *Daily News* reported that Broadway *Hair* was the "most dismaying low of the 1967-1968 season." It was "vulgar, perverted, tasteless, cheap, cynical, offensive, and generally lousy, and everybody connected with it should be washed in strong soap and hung up to dry in the sun."[80] Jack O'Brien's notice also dismissed the show as "a tangled mad-mod musical whose ultimate obscenities are not shocking though execrably tasteless, whose cast looks permanently bathless, whose points are not irreverent but sacrilegious; its hymns of 'love' are evilly hateful."[81] Even the *East Village Other* blasted the show. "*Hair* makes me sick . . . up here on stage for 2½ hours is an ersatz tribe of loving, rocking, musical, hairy quasi-hip people."[82] But the power of critics such as these was diminished by a new breed of reviewers, those appearing on local television, who uniformly loved the show and encouraged their viewers to see it ASAP. And the house was filled every night.

How far the Broadway establishment went in attempting to deny the existence of *Hair* is illustrated by an incident involving the League of New York Theatres and Producers. When producer Butler announced his intention to bring the musical to Broadway, he was assured by the League that if the show opened before a certain date the musical would be considered for the Tony Awards. When *Hair* met the condition, the League effectively reneged, proclaiming that works which did not originate on Broadway were ineligible for a Tony. Butler fought the decision and *Hair* was nominated for Best Musical. In the end the award went to *1776*, an expression of the League's conformist control.

On the other hand, some of the most conservative critics doffed their hats to the "rock 'n' rebellion" musical. Brooks Atkinson, dean of theater journalists, avowed that "*Hair* is the freshest and most spontaneous show I've seen."[83] Barnes loved the show, and as Richard Watts, Jr., of the *New York Post* described it, "*Hair* has surprising if perhaps unintentional charm; its high spirits are contagious, and its young zestfulness makes it difficult to resist."[84]

Was the Nudity Relevant?

Hair was the first show on Broadway to display totally naked actors and actresses.[85] Although the original script suggested a nude scene it was only at the Biltmore that the disrobing was sanctioned. Papp and Freedman chose not to recognize its relevance; neither did the Public version include the sexually explicit "Sodomy" or "The Bed." Indeed, some critics attributed the musical's Broadway success to the sensational publicity accorded the nude scene, and for many theatergoers, the presence of naked bodies on the Biltmore stage may well have been a magnetic attraction. Still, *Hair*'s prurient appeal was the target of many critics and patrons. During its first days, one could almost count on a handful of audience members leaving the theater during the Be-In sequence, several writing to the local press of their outrage at the obscene spectacle taking place at the Biltmore. But Mayor John Lindsay's police did not close the show, as Barnes had anticipated. Lindsay, who was a staunch supporter of theater, had been co-commissioner of the Kerner Commission, of which Butler was a member.

Although banned in Boston and Chattanooga, Supreme Court decisions upheld *Hair*'s First Amendment rights. By contemporary standards, the "naughty bits" seem like child's play, which they were. The scene at the end of the Be-In when the cast emerged from the scrim without their clothes, bathed in an overlay of floral patterned lighting, was considered by many, the creators included, as an esthetic moment, "selective . . . even discrete."[86]

Goldman, who thought the penis baring inappropriate, recalled a preview performance before the lights were dimmed for the esthetic moment. There it was "in all its Da Vincian glory . . . the cast a little edgy, standing there, limp penises and all. . . . And during the blackout, what you saw were these little naked gypsies, horrendously embarrassed, throwing their little hands across their fronts as they scurried madly off stage."[87]

Although the nudity was never mandated and no one was ever forced to strip, Joe Butler remembered powwow-business meetings with the cast sitting around in a circle, Big

Chief Michael Butler pontificating, wherein they "talked about extra money for nude pay."[88] Apparently, the tribe eventually "got with it," as did various uninhibited audience members who also discarded their clothes and jumped to the stage in the name of freedom.

Barnes thought the nudity was relevant.[89] Gottfried, on the other hand, confessed that he "just hated" the "flashing" on stage, adding that it caused many opening night spectators to squirm in their seats. Given the benefit of hindsight, he allowed "When I look back on it, it was important because they were intent on breaking the mold."[90] More than a decade later, Freedman's opinion did not falter. Asked if the nudity was barred at the Public to avoid conflict with the organization's sponsors, he objected: "Absolutely wrong, wrong, wrong. The nude scene wasn't included because it didn't make any sense. There were suggestions for it at the Be-In. The piece was supposed to be about freedom. It was eventually done under a net, under a red-flashing light, now you see it, now you don't. It was totally prurient. It had nothing to do with freedom."[91]

Was *Hair* Unpatriotic or Anti-American?

Many who caught wind of *Hair* chalked it up as a subversive, anti-American propaganda piece simply on the basis of its opposition to the war in Vietnam. But it was the erroneously perceived desecration of the flag scene that unleashed the greatest wrath of self-styled patriots. Joe Butler recalled two incidents in which the flag scene was interrupted by enraged patrons who jumped to the stage, one shouting, "You sons-a-bitches. If I had a machine gun. . . ."[92] On another occasion, astronauts James Lovell and John Swigert reportedly walked out of the Biltmore to the strains of "Don't Put It Down." Setting the record straight, neither Lovell nor Swigert left during the flag bit. One of them appeared on Forty-seventh Street during the intermission and made some disparaging remarks about the show before leaving altogether. The other remained for the second act. Even more intriguingly, the entire episode was videotaped. It appears that television news crews just happened to be on the scene, which does suggest the publicity stunt at the bottom of L'Affair *Hair*.[93]

Even if the astronaut story were accurate, Ragni and Rado insist that the flag was treated with due respect, that "Don't Put It Down" was a humorous homage to the flag, and that cast members were given explicit instructions to keep the flag from touching the ground.[94] Asked about the negative press that the show received as a result of the astronaut story, producer Michael Butler elaborated:

> It was just press. I had gone to a military academy. My background is the military-industrial establishment. I had a member of the General Staff in the audience on more than one occasion, colonels, generals, friends of mine who were military officers. They didn't see anything incorrect or wrong about the play. I purposefully invited them, because I did not want to do anything that would be considered insulting or improper to the flag, which I consider is the symbol of this country, even though I do agree with the artists' rights. If they want to "pee" on the flag, burn it, whatever, it is their right, but it's not what I choose to do.[95]

If *Hair*'s gentle protest against the war seemed unpatriotic, then *Hair*'s creators must plead *mea culpa*. It was, however, never their intent. The show was antiwar, never anti-American. The show simply pleaded for an awareness.

What about the Drugs?

Yes, drugs were a prominent part of *Hair*'s story, and whether the show legitimized or glamorized their usage, it seems incomprehensible that a musical about hippies could have avoided such references. During the LSD-trip sequence, the joints that Berger offered to cast members were at times the real stuff; and the stage directions include several references to various individuals either smoking pot or taking a drag.

But there is a backstage dimension to the *Hair*-drug connection, one that carried with it far darker and tragic dimensions. Lorrie Davis attested that she, and possibly Melba Moore, "was the only one in the show that didn't do any kind of illegal substance."[96] She attributed much of the "improvisation" on stage to the cast's use of drugs. To keep up the energy level, Dr. Bishop (also known as Dr. Feelgood and the Kennedys' doctor) administered shots of vitamins laced with methamphetamine on matinee Wednesdays. If you survived, an unidentified cast member disclosed, you went on to Dr. Jacobson. At twelve dollars a shot, Davis tried to negotiate the doctor's fee for extra pay, arguing unsuccessfully that that's what it would have cost management had she indulged.

Said Davis, it was a different show every night, because "you didn't know who was high, who was going to be sober, who was going to fall, or who was not going to show. That's what really made it a different show, because you were constantly dealing with these people."[97]

Although Davis and Joe Butler "stayed clean," many of the youthful cast could not resist the temptation. At least three members of the Biltmore cast, maybe more, succumbed to drug overdoses. Many became addicted, and many went into treatment programs. "I knew people had taken drugs, or had been drinking, but I didn't know the extent. When somebody told me, at the UN reunion, that she was in a program for a year, even though I know she did it, I didn't know that it had gotten out of hand."[98]

They were kids, fifteen, sixteen years old, but they weren't naive. They knew what they were doing. "I don't make excuses for others. I could have done drugs, been a hooker . . . the whole gamut, but I chose not to. They made their choices. That's what they did," said Davis. "I tried to tell them, but they wouldn't listen."[99] That drugs were a sign of the times, that *Hair* has wired for more than sound is clearly one of the unfortunate sides of the saga.

NOTES

1. Interview with James Rado, New York City, March 3, 1990.

2. Interview with Tom O'Horgan, New York City, November 4, 1977.

3. Lorrie Davis and Rachel Gallagher, *Letting Down My Hair* (New York: Arthur Fields, 1971), 13.

4. Oscar G. Brockett and Robert R. Findlay, *Century of Innovation: A History of European and American Theatre Since 1870* (Englewood Cliffs, N.J.: Prentice-Hall, 1973), 712.

5. Interview with Lorrie Davis, New York City, May 18, 1990.

6. Davis and Gallagher, 168.

7. Interview with Tom O'Horgan, New York City, April 13, 1990.

8. O'Horgan Interview, 1990.

9. Davis and Gallagher, 168.

10. Interview with James Rado, New York City, March 25, 1990.

11. Rado interview, March 25, 1990.

12. Interview with Joseph Campbell Butler, New York City, June 28, 1990.

13. Joseph Campbell Butler interview.

14. Joseph Campbell Butler interview.

15. Joseph Campbell Butler interview.

16. Joseph Campbell Butler interview.

17. Joseph Campbell Butler interview.

18. Joseph Campbell Butler interview.

19. Clive Barnes referred to Ragni as a psychedelic teddy bear in one of his reviews, and it was written into the opening monologue.

20. Davis interview.

21. Interview with Ellen Stewart, New York City, May 15, 1990.

22. Davis interview.

23. William Kloman, "*2001* and *Hair*—are They the Groove of the Future?" *The New York Times* (May 12, 1968): D8.

24. Interview with Gerald Freedman, New York City, October 27, 1977.

25. O'Horgan interview, 1990.

26. O'Horgan interview, 1977.

27. Interview with Clive Barnes, New York City, April 19, 1990.

28. Barnes interview.

29. Barnes interview.

30. Barnes interview.

31. William Goldman, *The Season: A Candid Look at Broadway* (New York: Harcourt, Brace & World, 1969), 383.

32. Gerome Ragni and James Rado, *"Hair:* The American Tribal Love–Rock Musical,'' in *Great Rock Musicals*, ed. Stanley Richards (New York: Stein and Day, 1979), 389.

33. Interview with Robin Wagner, New York City, June 19, 1981.

34. Interview with Jules Fisher, New York City, September 1, 1981.

35. Jules Fisher, *Hair*, Biltmore Souvenir Programs.

36. Robert Kotlowitz, *"Hair:* Side, Back and Front Views,'' *Harper's Magazine* (September 1968): 108.

37. Fisher interview.

38. The band was in the rafters at the Public. The stage was a double-decked arrangement.

39. Interview with Galt MacDermot, New York City, June 29, 1990.

40. Interview with James Rado, New York City, March 11, 1990.

41. O'Horgan interview, 1977.

42. Henry Hewes, "Blow-Ups," *Saturday Review* (May 11, 1968): 34.

43. Ronald Gold, "It's 'Non-Choreography,' but All Dance,'' *Dance Magazine* (July 1968): 29-30.

44. Nancy Potts, *Hair* Biltmore Souvenir Program.

45. Interview with Melba Moore, New York City, June 19, 1990.

46. Clives Barnes, "Theatre: Love-Rock Musical Initiates Playhouse,'' *The New York Times* (October 31, 1967): 55.

47. Eric Blau, *jacques brel is alive and well and living in paris* (New York: E. P. Dutton, 1971), 47.

48. O'Horgan interview, 1990.

49. Davis interview.

50. O'Horgan interview, 1990.

51. O'Horgan interview, 1990.

52. O'Horgan interview, 1990.

53. Brockett and Findlay, 713.

54. Clive Barnes, *"Hair," Saturday Evening Post* (September 8, 1977): 24.

55. Lehman Engel, *Words with Music* (New York: Macmillan, 1972), 301.

56. Interview with Martin Gottfried, New York City, April 19, 1990.

57. Rado interview, March 11, 1990.

58. Interview with Gerome Ragni and James Rado, New York City, March 25, 1990.

59. Ragni and Rado interview.

60. O'Horgan interview, 1990.

61. Harriet Deer and Irving Deer, Musical Comedy: From Performer to Performance, *Journal of Popular Culture* 12, no. 3 (Winter 1978): 406-417.

62. Gottfried interview.

63. Gottfried interview.

64. Gottfried interview.

65. Gottfried interview.

66. Gottfried interview.

67. Graham Vulliamy, "Music and the Mass Culture Debate," in *Whose Music?" A Sociology of Musical Languages*, Howard S. Becker, ed. (New Brunswick, N.J.: Transaction Press, 1977), 191.

68. John Rockwell, "Long Hair?" *Opera News* (December 20, 1969): 13.

69. MacDermot interview, 1990.

70. David Ewen, *The New Complete Book of the American Musical Theatre* (New York: Holt, Rinehart and Winston, 1970), 204.

71. Martin Gottfried, *Opening Nights: Theatre Criticism of the Sixties* (New York: G. P. Putnam, 1969), 103-105.

72. John S. Wilson, "Rock Goes the Musical Theatre," *The New York Times* (October 15, 1967). Clippings, Theatre Collection, New York Public Library.

73. Cited by Gottfried, *Words with Music*, 295.

74. Barnes interview.

75. Barnes interview.

76. MacDermot interview, 1990.

77. O'Horgan interview, 1990.

78. Gottfried interview.

79. Gottfried interview.

80. Goldman, 386.

81. Goldman, 386.

82. Goldman, 386.

83. Stanley Richards, ed., *Great Rock Musicals* (New York: Stein and Day, 1979), 381.

84. Richards, 381.

85. Kloman, D8.

86. Irving H. Buchen, "Is the Future *Hair*," *Journal of Popular Culture*, 3, no. 2 (Fall 1969): 324-332.

87. Goldman, 385.

88. Joseph Campbell Butler interview.

89. Barnes interview.

90. Gottfried interview.

91. Freedman interview, 1990.

92. Joseph Campbell Butler interview.

93. Abel Green, "L'Affair *Hair* and the Astronauts Who Walked Out," *Variety* (June 18, 1970): 65.

94. Interview with James Rado, New York City, March 25, 1990.

95. Interview with Michael Butler, New York City, April 3, 1990.

96. Davis interview.

97. Davis interview.

98. Davis interview.

99. Davis interview.

Chapter 5

Beyond Opening Night

All of the major critics came out to review *Hair* on Broadway, and again the reception was mixed. Some, however, dropped the earlier reservations they had about the downtown production, and now evaluated the piece as the best musical of the Broadway season.

Three members of the Critic's Circle—Clive Barnes, Henry Hewes, and Emory Lewis—voted *Hair* as the best musical of the year. Most of the critics were in agreement on one point—the excellence of the score. In *Variety*'s poll of eighteen New York drama critics, *Hair* won two awards: Ragni and Rado were elected best lyricists of the season with seven votes; MacDermot received the Drama Desk-Vernon Rice Award for his score.[1]

Barnes noted that the show had "landed, positively panting with love and smelling of sweat and flowers . . . so new, so fresh, and so unassuming, even in its pretensions . . . the frankest show in town."[2] Having received a number of letters from people who had seen previews asking him to warn his readers, or "in the urbanely quaint words of one correspondent, 'Spell out what is happening on stage,'" he confessed that he felt somewhat limited, since the *Times* was a family newspaper.[3] Adding to the favorable reviews, in the Sunday *Times*, Walter Kerr sought to allay fears of potential patrons:

"Yes, the din is dynamic, the stomp is perpetual, the put-on unflagging, the nudes are there. But there is no pressure to make you buy the bag, no *fear* in the performers. . . . They are simply beside you like bears going into your cabin in Yellowstone Park, soliciting love, causing no trouble, doing what they do. Occupying a lot of space but effortlessly belonging."[4]

Other critics were less tolerant with the revised *Hair* and its concentration on sensationalism. John Simon lamented, "As performed last fall at the off-Broadway Public Theater, *Hair* was an unpretentious, charming, swinging little musical. Not without flaws, it was youthful, zestful, tuneful and brimful of life. In this new Broadway version, it is merely fulsome . . . with shock and inoffensiveness as its contradictory aims."[5]

Most of the musical's commercial success on Broadway was due to promotional activities and exposure through the media, especially the television news. The television critics loved the show. Channel 2 reported that it was the "best musical of the year."[6] However, adroit press-agentry centered on two main newspaper quotes that said that *Hair* "makes *Marat/Sade* look like *Peter Pan*" and another that called it "the frankest show in town.' "[7]

Nine months after *Hair* opened at the Biltmore, Clive Barnes, a devotee of the show since its Public performance, stated that *Hair* remained "beautiful" on second viewing, for in his opinion, "it still seems as though the whole thing is swiftly, deftly, dazzlingly being improvised before your very eyes."[8] All three of the starring Broadway roles had been recast. Ragni and Rado had taken their roles to Los Angeles, the first production to be staged out of New York. Joseph Campbell Butler, former Lovin' Spoonful drummer-vocalist, assumed the part of Claude, recording artist Barry McGuire of "Eve of Destruction" fame took the role of Berger, and Heather MacRae replaced Lynn Kellogg as Sheila. In Barnes's view, this infusion of "new blood" helped to keep the show fresh and did not detract from the performance.

During its first two years on Broadway, all seemed well

with the show. In January 1970, RCA Victor announced the release of the Ragni, Rado, and MacDermot album entitled "DisinHairited." The heralded team had composed new songs for the album, demonstrating their ongoing creative talent. In April 1970, the management of *Hair* gave a free concert in Central Park to an audience of over 10,000. The birthday celebration was financed by the $2 million in profits which the musical had netted to that point. At this time, it appeared that the show might thrive on Broadway indefinitely.

But changes were beginning to take their inevitable toll. Most crucially, O'Horgan was now dividing his directorial talents between sporadic workshops for new members of the Broadway cast and *Hair* productions elsewhere. Davis observed, "when Tom O'Horgan left the show, what little discipline we had left with him."[9]

Less than a year after its Biltmore opening, Joseph Campbell Butler recalled that the Broadway *Hair* really didn't have a director. Instead the stage manager and choreographer Arenal provided whatever supervisory oversight there was. Without any stage background tribal chief Michael Butler took on directorial functions, devoting the bulk of his time to squabbling with Ragni and Rado, a situation that further exacerbated the tensions of a physical and mentally taxing show.[10]

The authors continued to garner new material from their observations, the workshop sessions, and the ad-libbing of new cast members in the New York production or in the various productions around the country. Fourteen sit-down companies ran concurrently with the Broadway show in various U.S. cities.[11] This contributed to a great deal of cross-fertilization, and a constant process of separating the wheat from the chaff. When the authors discovered something that worked, they were eager to write the bits into the Broadway show. Their insistence brought them into conflict with producer Butler, who at one point locked the authors out of the theater. "Butler saw the show as a finished product that worked," said Rado. "He didn't want any changes, rewrites, whatever. So he banned us from the theater. At one point, there were guards outside the Biltmore. 'Why mess with something that's working' was Butler's reasoning.''[12]

DOMESTIC PRODUCTIONS

The early success of *Hair* at the Biltmore encouraged Butler and O'Horgan to open road companies in various cities around the United States. The task of supervising such new companies fell to O'Horgan, who provided initial directorial input for the Los Angeles, San Francisco, and Chicago productions. Although some cast members from the Broadway show reprised their Biltmore roles in Los Angeles, San Francisco, Chicago, and elsewhere, the cast for the most part came from the city in which it was being performed. In each of these venues, the script was adapted to local circumstances. For example, on Broadway the actors would state that they were "going down to 42nd Street," which became Market Street in San Francisco and Michigan Avenue in Chicago.

In Los Angeles O'Horgan had access to a revolving stage, which added a new dimension to the show. While Ragni and Rado had come from the Broadway production, the rest of the ensemble was essentially a new acting company. When O'Horgan returned to New York, he took some of the new directorial ideas which evolved during the Los Angeles run and incorporated them into the Broadway performance.[13] Butler also went to Los Angeles, where he viewed a performance in which live chickens were tossed out onto the stage. When he returned to the Biltmore, he tried the chicken "bit," but it proved more of a distraction than an innovation. While some of *Hair*'s cross-fertilizations were effectively transposed, others were understandably dropped.

As an interesting aside, the Los Angeles production was performed at the newly named Aquarius Theatre. The show was a smash hit, and ran for nearly a thousand performances.

Before *Hair*, the longest run that a Broadway-based touring musical had ever achieved in Los Angeles was six months. *Hair* broke all records, playing for nearly three years.

The San Francisco production was O'Horgan's favorite. With its large hippie population, the city was a natural locale for the production, "an oasis of crazy cultural madness. . . . The audience was so with it. The flower children came wearing flowers."[14] The show began with the cast engaged in meditation. The audience would come up on stage and join in, and there would be "these big concentric circles of people meditating."[15] *Hair* was really an extension of the street activities of the hippies, and in a city like San Francisco, the barrier between art and life was often transcended.

While it was expected that *Hair* would be successful in New York, Los Angeles, San Francisco, and other hippie meccas, taking the show to the nation's capitol was a bit of a risk. *Hair* was targeted, after all, at aspects of government policy. Its reputation preceded it, and while it was there protest groups ranging from political organizations to the Smite Smut League and even the Gay Liberation Front picketed the theater.[16] On the other hand, many of the city's establishment notables attended *Hair* performances in Washington, including a bemused Henry Kissinger who reportedly enjoyed the show.[17]

The musical was staged in some of the more remote areas of the country, regions with little direct connection to the hippie movement. In St. Paul, concerned citizens rallied against the show, and tried unsuccessfully to ban it. On opening night, a frustrated clergyman released eighteen white mice into the lobby, hoping to frighten the audience. His actions went unnoticed, and the show enjoyed a warm reception in Minnesota.[18]

Opposition to the show in St. Paul was minimal compared to the legal furor created in Boston. Advance ticket sales were in excess of $600,000, and the show was slated to be a success—until a district attorney saw the show during previews.

Intent on preventing the opening performance, he finally agreed to suspend judgment until seven judges of the Massachusetts Supreme Court witnessed that which he held in evidence. After attending a preview performance, the judges concurred with the district attorney's decision.[19] A restraining order was issued. Hearings were held. The *Hair* company was given a date on the court calendar.

Clive Barnes recalled being brought in as an expert witness in defense of the *Hair* company. The district attorney duly recognized the theatrical expertise of Barnes, but questioned his credentials with respect to the prevailing community law in Boston.[20] The decision came down, and the company was ordered to make changes in the show before it could be performed in Boston. These changes included wearing some clothing during the nude scene and eliminating what was referred to as the "flag desecration" skit. The authors were willing to acquiesce, but producer Butler remained firm. He kept the cast on call, paying their expenses for more than a month, while the case was brought before the United States Supreme Court.[21] Nine judges of the country's highest tribunal overturned the decision of the Massachusetts judiciary, the majority opinion stating that such restrictions would have a "chilling effect on the right of free expression" guaranteed by the First Amendment.[22] Thus, the musical was staged in Boston without any alterations. The case was viewed as a landmark decision for freedom of expression in the American theater.

The issues which *Hair* raised came before the Supreme Court again, this time as the result of steps taken by officials in Chattanooga, Tennessee. The authorities there did not even permit preview performances, basing their ban solely on the musical's reputation.[23] The restraining order held for nearly three years as local authorities successfully delayed a second petition to the United States Supreme Court. In March 1975, the Court handed down a determination, maintaining that while *Hair* may have violated Chattanooga's prevailing standards of obscenity, the city's theater board had employed "unlawful prior restraint" when it denied *Hair* the use of its civic auditorium. "A free society," wrote Justice Harry Blackmun for the 5-to-4 majority, "prefers to punish the few who abuse rights of speech after they break the law rather than to throttle them and all others beforehand."[24]

As *Hair* reached out to its prospective national audience, it foreshortened its stay on Broadway. It wasn't necessary for audiences to come to New York to see the show, because the production was taken to them. The show was successful on the road in America, sit-down companies enjoying record-setting runs wherever they performed. On the road, *Hair* created controversies which could be resolved only by the highest judicial authority in the land. Had the show not encountered the resistance of the Bostons and the Chattanoogas, its importance as a piece that tested the permissible limits of free expression might have diminished. As it was, *Hair* not only enlightened and entertained audiences, it expanded the individual liberties of both theatergoers and nontheatergoers alike.

FOREIGN PRODUCTIONS

Executive producer Bertrand Castelli was the obvious choice to lead the foreign productions of *Hair*. After securing the foreign rights from Michael Butler and the authors, Castelli took an active part in shepherding the show around the world, producing and sometimes directing companies in France, Germany, Belgium, Italy, Japan, Mexico, and other countries. No stranger to innovation, Castelli elected to break with yet another time-honored Broadway tradition. "I decided to do it in the language of the country. At the time, Broadway shows were always done in English. So I did adaptations in German, French, Japanese, Spanish, Italian, Flemish, and many other tongues."[25]

While *Hair* became polyglot, Castelli followed the book. "The adaptations [translations] were very close to the English original. Nothing was changed. The same set was always used."[26] Isabelle Blau, a friend and an associate of Ragni and Rado since the early 1960s, represented the authors abroad as international production coordinator. She confirmed that while local adaptations were used, the basic Biltmore script remained intact, and the full panoply of O'Horgan-inspired techniques was utilized.[27] Each production had its own national accent: in England, the show was "sophisticated"; in Japan, it was "violent"; in Italy it was "jolly"; in Germany, "powerful."[28] Still, Butler complained that Castelli-inspired productions tended to be "anti-American in tone," introducing an element that ran contrary to the show's underlying intentions.[29] Despite the nuances, the performance that a German, a French, or a Japanese audience saw was basically identical to what their counterparts in New York, Los Angeles, or San Francisco saw.

Throughout his travels, Castelli encountered the same problems in casting. Given the language differences and variations in the availability of local talent, his task in finding amateur types to become members of the tribes was more difficult than was O'Horgan's. "In Germany, I saw 8,000 people; 5,000 in France; 3,000 in Japan; about 2,000 in London; in Mexico, about 500. It was a lot of work to find the people who could sing, and move, and at the same time possess the 'spirit.' The most difficult part was casting the show. When it was done, then it was easy."[30]

Hair was performed in nearly a score of foreign countries, and, as in the United States, reactions varied. In England, the musical circumvented the obscenity issue through a fortuitous circumstance. Immediately prior to its scheduled opening in the fall of 1968 at the Shaftesbury Theatre, the British Parliament eliminated the post of Lord Chamberlain, thereby dismantling the only legally constituted censorship office in the land.[31] One day after this action, *Hair* opened in London, avoiding the type of legal entanglement it would later confront in America. In any event, as was reported in a London daily, concern was not necessary since the majority of the company refused to disrobe voluntarily, believing that the show's nude sequence diluted its antiwar sentiments.[32] Sensitivities changed. O'Horgan, who directed the British production, recalled that audience members from Britain's film industry began to upstage their "legitimate" theater colleagues by coming onto the stage and taking off their clothes.[33]

Opening on September 27, 1968, the London *Hair* ran for 1,997 performances, outdistancing the Broadway run. Claude was portrayed by Paul Nicholas; Berger, by Oliver Tobias. As was the case in all the foreign productions, the London show had its sprinkling of local allusions and minor departures from the Broadway version. *Hair* was warmly received by its London audiences. When Princess Ann came to see the show, she is said to have enthusiastically joined the communal onstage activity that followed every performance, raising some royal eyebrows.[34]

In Paris, Castelli served as both director and producer. With the burdensome task of casting accomplished (5,000 performers auditioned for the 28 roles), the Paris production of *Hair* thrived. Barnes wrote that, "The Parisian *Hair* is perhaps the best, the hippest, and the happiest of them all."[35] Castelli had no problem convincing the Paris company of the relevance of the nude sequence: the cast disrobed on stage "almost religiously."[36] The Paris production was charged with local references. For instance, "when a Hippie distributes LSD sugar cubes, he says, 'Here's one for François Mauriac, one for Tante Yvonne (the nickname for Charles de Gaulle's spouse), and one for Madame Pompidou'—and that brings down the house."[37]

Even in Paris, however, the musical was not without its opponents. In one amusing episode, a contingent of the local Salvation Army came to view a performance. During the pseudo-religious episode, featuring a crucifix, Commander Gilbert Abadie used a portable loudspeaker to exhort the crowd to halt the presentation.[38]

The cast objected to Jacques Landsman's translation of "Easy to Be Hard." It had a negative slant, which gave the hippies a hard stance. Through Blau's intervention, the lyrics were softened to suit the Parisian tribe's demands.[39]

Whereas the London and Paris productions were the most noteworthy of the stagings abroad, they were preceded by openings in other European cities. One week before its London debut, the show opened in Stockholm. Given Sweden's reputation for sexual freedom, there was surprising reluctance by the Stockholm company to appear unclothed on stage. Moreover, Julie Arenal found her Swedish dancers uncomfortable with the American style of dancing. Consequently, she was forced to work long hours to reshape the dance movements. In Bergen, Norway, the local citizenry formed a human barricade to prevent (unsuccessfully) the performance, the townspeople viewing it as a "brutalizing spectacle."[40] On the other hand, in Copenhagen, the Danish company felt that the mild nudity had insufficient shock value. Some of the tribe went *au naturel* during the opening sequence, walking down the aisles of the theater and mingling with the audience en route to the stage.[41] During the Be-In sequence where the nudity called for the tribe to remain motionless, the tribe disrobed and danced freely. Naked audience members enthusiastically took to the stage to join in the celebration, and the Be-In was extended to a full ten minutes.[42] Thus, while some Scandinavians found *Hair*'s sexual license too much to accept, others found it too mild, and the show adapted to decidedly local mores. (The Stockholm, Bergen, and Copenhagen productions were directed by local directors.)

In Munich, Germany, where Castelli again directed, authorities threatened to close the show if the nude sequence remained. Castelli proved more than equal to this challenge.

A spokesman for the local impresario replied that his relatives had been nude when marched into Auschwitz.[43] The entirely nude tribe covered themselves during the nude Be-In with a large banner that stretched the length of the stage. It listed all of Germany's World War II abbattoir. The nude scene was permitted on the following night until the end of the run. No further executive murmurs were uttered.[44]

Another ineffectual effort to close *Hair* was made by the Protestant ministry in Montreux, Switzerland, a conservative community which viewed the work as a scandal.[45]

At a time known behind the now-crumbled Iron Curtain as the "Prague spring," a most unusual and successful production took place in Belgrade, Yugoslavia. It was directed by a local female director. As described in *Newsweek*, the Yugoslavian version was a delight for both audience and company. The authors attended a performance of *Kosa*, as *Hair* was billed in Belgrade. The production remained one of their favorites. "So beautiful, so spontaneous" was the show that they climbed to the stage to share the enthusiasm by singing along in the title song "Hair." "Said Medusa-haired Ragni, 'there's no middleclass prejudice here.'"[46] One patron of the Belgrade show who reportedly enjoyed himself was Josef Broz, also known as Marshal Tito.[47] Local references were introduced into the performance. There were barbs aimed not only at Mao Ze-dong, but also at Yugoslavia's traditional enemy, Albania.[48] On the other hand the issue of draft-dodging in America was disregarded, probably because most Yugoslav youth felt it was honorable to serve in the national armed forces, particularly one committed to maintaining independence from the Soviet Union.

The show was favorably received in countries of the British Commonwealth, most especially Australia (staged by Jim Sharman, who had directed the Boston production) and Canada. The Toronto production was co-directed by Ragni and Rado, the only version of *Hair* directed by its authors. Julie Arenal accompanied the authors to Toronto, where she was favorably impressed with the talent and vivacity of her dancers. For the Toronto show, Ragni and Rado teamed with MacDermot to compose another tune, "So Sing the Children on the Avenue."[49]

In June 1969, *Hair* opened in Sydney, Australia.[50] The production was enthusiastically greeted by audience and critics alike, and the reaction to the nude sequence was, in general, far more sympathetic than in some United States cities. Nudity was seen by the Australian audiences as a legitimate form of youthful expression, and the Australian directors did not have to urge their casts to disrobe. Eventually, members of the Australian cast and crew took part in the productions staged in the Philippines and the concert version in Vietnam.

The show did not enjoy a similar welcome in Acapulco, Mexico. There authorities closed the piece after a single performance.[51] Ragni and Rado were among the audience members on opening night, as was the daughter of the Mexican president.[52] This would be the one and only Mexican performance of *Hair* in 1969, for that night after the show, Mexican authorities secured a thick wooden bar to the theater's door. At seven the next morning, the cast and crew were rounded up, hauled off to jail, and given a choice: either leave Mexico at once or stay and face criminal charges.[53] Unsure of their legal position, the members of the Mexican company, many of whom had been in the Los Angeles show, decided to quit Acapulco, a move which was seconded by the Mexican Actors Association.[54] Ragni and Rado were less fortunate. They were given no options. Hiding out in a local hacienda in the hills, they learned via the radio that they were being sought for questioning. A local dragnet had been set up to "capture them at the airport." Through the help of friends in the local "underground," they were "smuggled to the airport in Mexico City," thus escaping the unspecified charges.[55]

As a postscript, the Acapulco producer, Alfred Quiez, revived the idea of mounting a Mexican production in Mexico

City at a later date. Quiez was ultimately replaced by Joseph Donovan, a longtime friend of Ragni's. After some touch-and-go negotiations with the national censorship board with Isabelle Blau mediating, *Hair* was staged in Mexico City in 1975. The nude Be-In remained.[56]

"Argentina was scary," said Blau. Aside from the unusual censorship, the ruling military junta cracked down on all hippies, which they considered to be drug-crazed, leftist subversives. This included the long-haired tribe members who had been cast from the Buenos Aires area.[57] While away from the theater, cast members, still highly visible in their hippie garb and long hair, were frequently arrested, detained, and, on occasion, beaten by the Peronist police.[58] The final approval for *Hair*'s staging in Buenos Aires came only after a Catholic priest attended a preview. The theologian, worldly by Latin American standards (he had reportedly seen the Paris production) consented to the piece, nudity and all.[59]

Japan was an unusual setting for *Hair*. Under the supervision of Japanese entrepreneur Shotaro Kawazoe and Shirley MacLaine's husband, Steve Parker, who was also one of the producers, the show did well. The dim lighting of the nude sequence obviated the problem of censorship. One of the most successful of the foreign stagings, *Hair* was performed atop a midtown department store. Each performance in Tokyo included a policeman, stationed in the wings, to ensure that no bright lights would illuminate the spectacle of the nude scene.[60] With major Japanese recording stars in the lead roles, Blau remembers the Tokyo production as being especially moving, commenting that the normally disciplined and impassive Japanese audiences were visibly touched by the performances.[61] Of the eleven original cast albums that were cut, the Japanese cast recording ranks at the top in its expression of the sensibilities of the culture. It is replete with Far Eastern instrumentation.

Hair underwent still other experiences abroad which have not been fully documented. In Rome, *Hair* was first shown in the summer of 1970, meeting with distinct indifference at this late date.[62] In Spain, Butler found a Madrid company performing an unauthorized version of the show, and the bogus production was soon closed by the Franco government.[63]

In what was perhaps the boldest of moves, Castelli marshalled members from the Philippines band and toured the U.S. bases in Vietnam. Military authorities were not about to allow a full-scale production of the show, but they did allow the company to perform the English language renditions of the show's tunes, and Castelli remembers the tour as being very successful.[64]

In general, *Hair* did well abroad. Performed in over a dozen languages in national climates ranging from liberal to repressed, the universality of its message transcended cultural boundaries.

THE 1977 BROADWAY REVIVAL

Much of *Hair*'s impact and appeal was the result of its reflection of an ongoing contemporary social phenomenon, the hippie counterculture of the late 1960s and 1970s. By the 1970s the hippies had faded from the scene, yet the members of the Broadway creative team collaborated again on a revival of the musical at the Biltmore. Butler (producer), O'Horgan (director), MacDermot (musical director), Arenal (dance director), Wagner (scenic designer), Fisher (lighting designer), and Potts (costume designer) were all involved in the enterprise, as were Ragni and Rado, playing minor parts as the bogus policemen who "bust" the show during the nude sequence. The show opened on October 5, 1977, just five years after the original Broadway closing, in what lingers on as *Hair*'s darkest hour. Perhaps, the producer should have taken his cues from the 1974 London revival at the Queen's Theatre, wherein MacDermot's enduring score was praised, but most critics concurred that *Hair*'s material was no longer timely, its themes no longer controversial, its efforts at updating transparent and ludicrous.[65]

Backstage, *Hair* 1977 was filled with familiar faces, but in front of the footlights, the leads and tribe members were entirely new. Randall Easterbrook was cast as Claude, Michael Hoit played Berger, and the part of Sheila went to Ellen Foley. The secondary leads of Woof, Hud, Jeanie, and Crissy were performed, respectively, by Scott Thornton, Cleavant Derricks, Iris Rosenkrantz, and Kriston Vigard.[66] (A complete listing of the cast and staff of the 1977 show appears in Appendix C.) Of the twenty-six cast members, only four, David Patrick Kelly, Toni Moreno, Alaina Reed, and Jim Sbano had previously appeared in a version of *Hair*.[67]

Whether to stage the Biltmore script or to revise and update the material was debated. Butler opted for a replica in his typical "if it works, why change it" rationale. The authors agreed, although they felt the need for new material.[68] O'Horgan found himself in the peculiar position of trying to remember the details of the earlier production, working rather mechanically from preset ideas, rather than from the spontaneity and collective contributions of the cast. New songs managed to get into the production, but the creative team blundered into a conservative compromise that left no one happy, not even the audiences.

A half-hearted attempt to make the musical topically relevant was made. References to Anita Bryant, Reverend Moon, Idi Amin, Andrea McCardle, and Crazy Eddie were included. During the protest march scene, the tribe carried signs with topical messages such "No Nukes Is Good Nukes," "Con Ed Goofed," and "Save the Whales."[69] Sheila became a representative of the women's movement. With all the attempts to update, the 1977 production included the focus on the Vietnam War, the customary hippie paraphernalia—strobe lights, flowers, electronic rock, and ragas, and all of the basic accoutrements of the previous decade: a curious admixture of a 1970s patina grafted onto a body that was still stuck in the sixties.

The revival ran for 79 previews and a total of 43 post-opening performances.[70] It met with almost universal revilement, and even easygoing Galt MacDermot was compelled to admit that "it just wasn't a good production."[71] *Hair* in 1977 was in chronological limbo, too old to be socially relevant and too recent to be staged as a museum piece. Of course, when a piece is brought back too soon after its closing, there is the natural tendency to compare the production to the past. This predisposition may have had some influence on those viewing the 1977 production.

The authors said casting was the primary obstacle to the revival's success. The charismatic personalities of the past with their social convictions were just not to be found at the time. It wasn't a matter of talent, it was just that the actors externalized hippie behavior, simply mimicking stage actions that they thought were appropriate.[72] Original cast member Lorrie Davis also identified casting as the "big mistake" in the revival production, the hiring of "talent" as opposed to O'Horgan's search for "personalities" in 1968.[73] The director himself began to have misgivings in this early workshops. He found that the new cast simply took directions without question or heated debate, and gone was the 1968 penchant for arguing over character interpretation and thematic significance.[74]

The question of talent apart, it seems evident that the 1977 cast relied on a professional distancing from the material, a disciplined and objective approach which ran counter to the uninhibited spontaneity that spoke of *Hair*'s success when originally staged on Broadway.

TRANSPOSITION TO FILM

In 1978, work was begun on adapting *Hair* for a motion picture, and a completed film was released in March 1979. The film was produced by Lester Persky and Michael Butler, and directed by Milos Forman, who brought with him two long-time associates, veteran cinematographer Miroslav Ondricek and accomplished screenplay writer Michael Weller. Choreography was assigned to young and talented

Twyla Tharp. Galt MacDermot served as musical director. John Savage, Treat Williams, and Beverly D'Angelo headed the cast as Claude, Berger, and Sheila. None of the leads had yet achieved the fame that would accrue to them in the 1980s, which was actually an advantage: each was extraordinarily gifted, but none had developed a film persona that might otherwise undermine their credibility in their character portrayals. The minor leads of Hud, Woof, and Jeanie were performed by Dorsey Wright, Don Dacus, and Annie Golden. The part of Crissy was cut. (A complete list of the staff and cast of the film is presented in Appendix D.)

The story of how Milos Forman came to direct the film version of *Hair* is almost as intriguing as the tale of how the show became a Broadway hit. Forman saw the first preview at the Public Theater in the fall of 1967. Struck by the power of the piece, he went backstage that night and asked the authors for a copy of the script, promising that he would write a review upon returning to his native Prague. Back in Czechoslovakia, Forman tried to interest local producers in mounting a production of *Hair*, but met with the same opposition that Castelli would later encounter. The musical was far too subversive to pass muster with the Communist Party.

Forman returned to the United States and met with Ragni and Rado. He wanted *Hair* to be his first American film. The authors admired Forman's Czech films, especially *Loves of a Blond* and *The Fireman's Ball*. Yet, while Forman was recognized as a top director in international film circles and by a small coterie of film aficionados here in the United States, his name carried little weight in Hollywood. By contrast, *Hair* was rapidly becoming a household word, a synonym for *hippies* even to those who had never seen the show. Commercial sense dictated that it would be a mistake to couple the "hot property" with a director with little marquee power. Disappointed, Forman did the next best thing. He directed the antiestablishment piece *Taking Off*, a modestly successful film that he would later describe as his story for *Hair*.[75]

Meanwhile, with *Hair*'s prospective worth as a film sky-

rocketing, Ragni and Rado were approached by Columbia
Pictures Executive Producer Gerald Ayres in 1979, who presented them with a "fabulous offer" which in hindsight they
wish they had accepted.[76] Many considerations tempered
their decision to turn down Ayres's proposal, but they really
wanted Milos Forman to direct the film. Torn between putting *Hair* on the screen immediately or waiting for Forman to
become a bankable entity, Ragni and Rado stood pat.[77]
When Forman's enormously successful adaptation of Ken
Kesey's *One Flew Over the Cuckoo's Nest* compelled Hollywood to take notice of the upstart Czech director, it appeared
that the authors had made a prescient choice.

Withholding the film rights until Michael Butler acquired
them with Lester Persky, Ragni and Rado were thrilled to
have Forman named as director for the cinematic version of
"their baby." However, the elation subsided as things went
steadily downhill. Ragni and Rado had written their own
screenplay, but at Persky's insistence, Forman brought in the
more experienced Michael Weller to author the decidedly different film treatment. Glancing over the Weller script, Ragni
and Rado were by no means content with the adaptation, and
they were even less happy with the finished product. Faced
with the opinion of seasoned movie veterans, they capitulated
to their "greater film wisdom," trusting in Forman to bring
the project to fruition.[78]

Transposing *Hair* to film afforded the director opportunities not available to O'Horgan. He could vary perspective
and focal length; he could reshoot scenes; he could edit his
takes; and he could employ dazzling techniques. The production, a painstaking labor that took almost a year, went forward with a thirty-seven-to-one film ratio.[79] It featured both
rapid cutting and the liberal use of montage. Calling on
Ondricek's expertise, a number of visual ingenuities were employed, especially in recreating *Hair*'s hallucinatory scenes.
Al Auster praised the film as a "visually beautiful" work.[80]

In its original form, *Hair* had a self-reflective theatricality.

The book contains several references that depend on a conscious undermining of the theatrical illusion. For example, when Berger asks Sheila why she's always making posters, she responds that the posters are "for the end of the show." At another juncture, Woof complains, "If I hear Vietnam one more time, I'm leaving this theatre." While such amusing adjuncts to *Hair*'s broad assault on the fourth wall worked in a stage context, they were inappropriate to the realistic treatment of the film. References to the work as a stage piece had to be cut from the film. But the changes which Forman made were not simply deleting a few lines of dialogue.

Had Forman confined his revision to an exploitation of cinematic techniques and the blotting of a line of dialogue here and there, a relatively faithful account of the stage production might have been realized. But Forman did not stop there. Explaining the extent of his revisions, Forman stated "*Hair* was such a brilliant piece of theatrical genius that you have only two ways how to make a film out of it, either photograph the stage play faithfully or let me make, absolutely free, my own version."[81] Although Forman admits that he could have taken the first course if the authors insisted, he chose the second option, making extensive changes from the original book.

One area in which Forman attempted to remain faithful to the original Broadway version was its musical numbers. One or two songs were added by MacDermot, Ragni, and Rado, but they were employed as source music, "not as upfront muscial numbers."[82] MacDermot did all the orchestration for the film. Tharp's choreography enhanced the show's gymnastics. About one-half of the finished production was devoted to the musical numbers that previously appeared in the Biltmore program. However, "Frank Mills," "I Believe in Love," "Don't Put It Down," "Going Down," "My Conviction," "Air," "The Bed," and "What a Piece of Work Is Man"—nearly a third of the Biltmore score—was deleted. In addition, "Walking in Space" and "Three-Five-Zero-

Zero'' were reduced to background pieces accompanying a slapstick review of the troops at an army boot camp.[83]

In terms of structure, Forman made considerable changes, giving the work a comparatively coherent plot. The film opens with Claude (John Savage) leaving his home in the Midwest to attend an induction physical in New York. In Forman's version Claude is no longer an aspiring hippie film student who lives with Berger and Sheila in an East Village flophouse. He's a genuinely typical, naive American youth who hasn't a clue as to what the hippies are all about. He comes from a ranch in Oklahoma and almost immediately wanders into a Central Park Be-In, a seemingly endless happening to which the camera returns again and again, where he meets Berger and the other members of the tribe. Berger initiates Claude into the joys of the counterculture, a lifestyle that Claude embraces without hesitation. He meets Sheila, who is no longer an NYU student/antiwar protestor, but a Long Island society debutante. It is not Berger's cajolings, but true emotional attachment, that causes her to become romantically interested in Claude, the cowboy from Oklahoma. Sheila's newly acquired status permits Forman to include a lengthy sequence in which Berger and the tribe invade a posh birthday party given for her, with Berger dancing on tables and performing other *epater les bourgeois* antics to the chagrin of the guests. Berger no longer resembles a hippie. "He is closer to being a madcap village idiot than a representative of the hippies."[84] Berger eventually devises a means for helping his now-bosom companion evade the draft. He will temporarily assume Claude's place at the army barracks. Predictably, the ruse backfires, and Berger, not Claude, is shipped to Vietnam to be killed.

Forman loaded his version of *Hair* with complex contrasts in character and ironic twists in narrative development that have no counterparts in the stage piece. In terms of structure, Forman's film has a much more complicated and coherent form than that of the Broadway musical. The setting of the original *Hair* was highly localized with numerous references to the East Village as the scene of the musical's action. Forman opens up the script, moving from Oklahoma to New York and back to Nevada, as the group sets out to rescue Claude from the military. The trip out west in a Lincoln Continental is filled with characters of every age, race, and socioeconomic standing, a black lady and her child, the newly liberated debutante from Long Island, the dropout from a lower-middle class home in Flushing, Queens, and some characters who appear to have wandered in from the set of another movie. "It's a real ethnic arc. In the original *Hair* the thing that all the street people had in common was their rootlessness. No one had a home or a background."[85] In the film, major characters have offscreen homes, and the geographical expansion of plot seems an effort to connect the hippies with America at large.[86]

The transnational feature of the Forman film can be interpreted as an attempt to divest the characters of their highly localized origins in the East Village. The song "Frank Mills" may have been dropped from the movie because it contained specific allusions to the streets of the West Village "outside the Waverly." This, of course, would increase the degree of identification that movie audiences outside of New York could extend to the characters in the film. Whether the purpose was to provide varied backgrounds or remove the local background, the effect was the same, with Forman transforming the piece into an America-wide spectacle that included shadings of various socioeconomic backgrounds in contrast to the hippie/straight dichotomy of the original stage piece.

The characterizations in the Broadway *Hair* were obviously biased toward the hippies, whose vitality and innocence were juxtaposed against the materialism and absurdity of the parent culture. In the movie, the hippies are "both innocent and selfish, sweet and surly, peace-loving and disruptive."[87]

What is most acutely absent from the film's pan-American excursion is the spirit that gave *Hair* its overwhelming impact on Broadway and propelled it on its journey to theaters around the world. "It seems that Milos Forman regarded the hippies as some sort of aberration," Rado would lament. Rado saw them portrayed simply as "oddballs," without any understanding of their motives, their search for truth, their commitment to the peace-love movement, their efforts to create a world based on human values.[88]

Ironically, what was a genuine revolution on the stage devolved into a hackneyed adaptation on the screen. Measuring their displeasure, Ragni and Rado confided that they refer to the film as *H* because Forman took all of the *air* out of *Hair*.[89] "Any resemblance between the 1979 film and the original Biltmore version, other than *some* of the songs, the names of the characters, and a common title, eludes us."[90] In their view, Forman was not able to come up with a form that matched the revolutionary content. In their view, a celluloid recording of the stage version would have been better than what transpired. In their view, a screen version of *Hair* has yet to be made. (As a postscript: Butler says the investors have never seen a dime from the film.)

RECENT REVIVALS

On May 26, 1988, a gala concert dinner version of *Hair* was presented at the General Assembly Hall of the United Nations. The elegant black tie affair was sponsored by the Creo Society, under the honorary chairmanship of First Lady Nancy Reagan, King Juan Carlos I and Queen Sophia of Spain, and the Secretary General of the United Nations and Mrs. Javier Perez de Cuellar. The event which celebrated the twentieth anniversary of the show's appearance on Broadway, reunited original cast members and their successors who were flown in from around the world to appear in a program that featured the now-classic *Hair* tunes plus a sampling of the creators' soon-to-be-produced *Sun*. The UN affair was a benefit performance, the proceeds of which went to the Fund for Children with AIDS. The Assembly Hall was filled to capacity. Ticket prices ranged from $250 to $5,000. Dinner was served after the performance.

Barbara Walters introduced the evening's festivities. Among the guest performers were Bea Arthur (who sang "Black Boys" with a new stanza added), Nell Carter, Frank Stallone (brother of Sylvester), Donna Summers, Treat Williams, and Dr. Ruth Westheimer playing Margaret Meade, speaking the dialogue that leads to "My Conviction."

"The best part of the reunion," says Lorrie Davis, "was seeing the other members of the tribe, like Natalie [Mosco] who came in from Australia. Even Sally Eaton. I mean it was great seeing those people, because we had some fabulous times."[91] Melba Moore also fondly remembers being moved at the sight of her old cohorts, recalling *Hair* as "the first experience she had working with strangers in this kind of a laboratory environment where the rule of thumb," in spite of the occasional bickering, "was really a loving environment."[92]

Since the widely publicized United Nations concert there has been a rekindled interest in the rock musical of the sixties. In November 1988, a Chicago production that also commemorated the twentieth anniversary was staged by Butler for an open run at the Vic Theatre. Well-received by critics and audiences alike, it ran until February 1989.[93] In the beginning of 1989, *Hair* was presented at the Performance Studio in New Haven.[94] By March, Fort Lauderdale had gotten on the *Hair* bandwagon, Ragni and Rado jumping aboard to rewrite and try out new scenes and songs.[95] A snowball effect was apparent when a Miami Beach producer saw the Fort Lauderdale show and committed her organization to a month-long staging of *Hair* scheduled to coincide with the twentieth anniversary of the Woodstock music festival.[96]

In May 1989, a Bridgeport, Connecticut, production was directed by Stanley Ramsey, a former tribe member and Hud understudy from the 1970 Biltmore cast. Wondering just how revolutionary the piece would be to modern audiences, executive producer Richard C. Hallinan justified his decision: "Yes, *Hair* is obviously dated. The spector of AIDS and the pressing problem of drugs make it so. But we're trying to make a virtue of the period and keep to it. This is the way it was and this is the way it looked."[97] After seeing the Chicago production, Hallinan realized that there was a whole new generation who had never heard the songs or seen the stage production. "I've always loved the music, and its infectious enthusiasm. I know its old, but right now it's all fresh and new to me. And this was the first time young people dared to get up and challenge the establishment."[98]

Ramsey used sensitivity and trust exercises and other experimental techniques that he had learned from Broadway director O'Horgan. "As for research, each cast member was asked to fill out a thirty-six part questionnaire that asked such questions as 'Where is Woodstock?' 'What was Kent State?' 'Who was Janis Joplin?' and 'How long was the U.S. Vietnam involvement?' "[99]

In September 1990, Pink Lace Productions began a non-equity bus and truck tour of one-night stands at major houses across the country. Constantly on the move, the troupe staged six performances a week. The company, which was put together in New York City, opened in Pennsylvania (Reading), and then went to Massachusetts, Vermont, New Hampshire, New York, Connecticut, Rhode Island, Maine, and Ontario. They played a good part of Florida, Tennessee, Georgia, South Carolina, Louisiana, Kentucky, Maryland, Delaware, and Virginia before moving to the West Coast. The tour concluded March 3, 1991.

Inspired by the renewed interest in *Hair*, and recognizing a window of opportunity in the American public's growing fascination with the 1960s, Ragni and Rado teamed with Mac-Dermot to completely revamp their show into what they call "the new and revised *Hair*." The 1990 version contains two new songs, "The Vietnam Song," and "Hippie Life," new lyrics to other songs, new instrumental music for the rewritten war sequence, and a major restructuring of the other scenes. Having fine-tuned the show, the authors are confident that they have at last come up with the definitive script for *Hair*.

Select theater groups have already been permitted to stage the newest version. It was first presented at a theater in Framingham, Massachusetts, in the summer of 1988, and followed by productions in Boulder, Colorado, and Woodstock, New York, in 1989. In conjunction with Bertrand Castelli, the authors have most recently prepared a Russian translation of the newest version of *Hair* for ultimate transport to Moscow. Although scheduling has not gone according to plan (repatriating profits from a country that lacks a convertible currency being a major issue), the irrepressible optimist Castelli still sees the Soviet Union as a platform for the latest revised *Hair*, in a campaign that will cross several international borders. As he says, "The piece is very relevant. The freedom. The spirit of rebellion that is taking place all over Europe in the name of freedom rather than the war."[100] Asked about further plans, Castelli waxed enthusiastic. "Yes, I would like to do it in Germany and Berlin, the city of the fall of the wall, a production in France and in Spain, and then I would like to do the newest version of *Hair* all around America, back on Broadway—to use the power of the show to again say things—social, political."[101] With the current state of international affairs, all plans have been put on hold.

NOTES

1. Abe Laufe, *Broadway's Greatest Musicals* (New York: Funk & Wagnalls, 1969), pp. 358-359.

2. Clive Barnes, "Theater: *Hair*—It's Fresh and Frank; Likable Rock Musical Moves to Broadway." *The New York Times* (April 30, 1968). Clippings, Theatre Collection, New York Public Library.

3. Barnes.

4. Walter Kerr, "*Hair*: Not in Fear, but in Delight," *The New York Times* (May 19, 1968): D3.

5. John Simon, *Uneasy Stages: A Chronicle of the New York Theatre, 1963-1973* (New York: Random House, 1975), 141.

6. William Goldman, *The Season: A Candid Look at Broadway* (New York: Harcourt, Brace & World, 1969), 384-385.

7. Goldman, 384-385.

8. Clive Barnes, "*Hair* Holds up Under 2d Look," *The New York Times* (February 5, 1969): 36.

9. Lorrie Davis and Rachel Gallagher, *Letting Down My Hair* (New York: Arthur Fields, 1971), 201.

10. Interview with Joseph Campbell Butler, New York City, June 28, 1990.

11. Stanley Richards, ed., *Great Rock Musicals* (New York: Stein and Day, 1979), 381.

12. Interview with Gerome Ragni, New York City, March 3, 1990.

13. Davis and Gallagher, 213.

14. Nahma Sandrow, "What Will *Hair* Say to the 70s?" *The New York Times* (October 2, 1977): D26.

15. Sandrow, D26.

16. Colette Dowling, "How *Hair* Found Fame and Fortune," *Playbill* (September 1968): 20.

17. Dowling, 20.

18. Dowling, 20.

19. Laufe, 362.

20. Interview with Clive Barnes, New York City, April. 19, 1990.

21. "Supreme Court Clears *Hair* for Boston Run," *The New York Times* (May 23, 1970): C27.

22. "Uncut '*Hair*' Reopens in Boston, Saved by Supreme Court Ruling," *Variety* May 27, 1970): 57.

23. William K. Warren, "Attorney for *Hair* Irks Judge with Comments on Scopes Trial," *Chattanooga Times* (April 5, 1973): 1.

24. "Supreme Court: Letting the Sun Shine In," *Newsweek* (March 31, 1975): 37.

25. Interview with Bertrand Castelli, New York City, March 6, 1990.

26. Castelli interview.

27. Interview with Isabelle Blau, New York City, March 31, 1990.

28. Castelli interview.

29. Interview with Michael Butler, New York City, April 3, 1990.

30. Castelli interview.

31. "Exit the Censor," *The Christian Scientist Monitor* (October 5, 1968): 18.

32. Kevin D'Arcy, "A Little Nudity Sells a Lot of Tickets," *London Sunday Telegraph* (September 29, 1969): 17.

33. Interview with Tom O'Horgan, New York City, April 13, 1990.

34. William Glover, "*Hair* Is a Continuous Happening," *New York Sunday News* (August 2, 1970), E4.

35. Clive Barnes, "New *Hair*," *The New York Times* (September 13, 1969): 30.

36. "*Hair* around the World," *Newsweek* (July 7, 1979): 94. Clippings, Theatre Collection, New York Public Library.

37. "*Hair* around the World," 94.

38. John L. Hess, "Salvation Army Jousts with *Hair* in Paris," *The New York Times* (February 2, 1970). Clippings, Theatre Collection, New York Public Library.

39. Blau interview.

40. Glover, E4.

41. Dowling, 32.

42. Interview with James Rado, New York City, March 25, 1990.

43. Glover, E4.

44. Glover, E4.

45. Gene Lees, "*Hair* in Europe," *Hi Fidelity* (June 1970): 108.

46. "*Hair* around the World," 94.

47. Glover, E4.

48. *Newsweek* (July 17, 1969): 94.

49. Clive Barnes, "Untitled," *The New York Times* (January 13, 1970): C26.

50. "*Hair* Reaches Australia," *The New York Times* (June 7, 1969): C26.

51. "Mexico Shuts *Hair* and Expels Its Cast After One Showing," *The New York Times* (January 1969): C43.

52. Rado interview.

53. Dowling, p. 32.

54. "Mexican Actors Favor *Hair* Cast Deportation," *The New York Times* (January 8, 1969): C35.

55. Rado interview.

56. Blau interview.

57. Blau interview.

58. Blau interview.

59. Blau interview.

60. Blau interview.

61. Blau interview.

62. Robert Ghisays, "Rome Test: Bracing for *Hair*," *The Newark Evening News* (August 30, 1970): 46.

63. "Assert Madrid *Hair* Was Pirate Version," *Variety* (August 19, 1970).

64. Castelli interview.

65. Frank Marcus, "Graying *Hair*," *London Sunday Telegraph* (June 30, 1974).

66. John Willis, *Theatre World: 1977-1978 Season* (New York: Crown, 1979), 26.

67. William Harris, "*Hair* Transplant," *Soho Weekly News* (September 8, 1977): 26.

68. Interview with Gerome Ragni and James Rado, New York City, March 11, 1990.

69. Sandrow, D26.

70. Willis, 42.

71. Interview with Galt MacDermot, New York City, August 11, 1990.

72. Rado interview.

73. Interview with Lorrie Davis, New York City, May 18, 1990.

74. Interview with Tom O'Horgan, New York City, April 13, 1990.

75. Todd McCarthy, "Milos Forman Lets Down His *Hair*," *Film Comment* (March-April 1979): 19.

76. Rado interview.

77. Rado interview.

78. Rado interview.

79. McCarthy, 19.

80. Al Auster, "*Hair*," *Cineaste* (Spring 1979): 55.

81. McCarthy, 18.

82. McCarthy, 18.

83. Colin L. Westbrook, "*Hair* Today," *Commonwealth* (May 25, 1979): 306.

84. Interview with Gerome Ragni, New York City, March 3, 1990.

85. Westbrook, 305, 306.

86. Westbrook, 305, 306.

87. David Denby, "*Hair* Transplanted," *New York* (March 29, 1979): 62.

88. Rado interview.

89. Ragni and Rado interview.

90. Ragni and Rado interview.

91. Davis interview.

92. Interview with Melba Moore, New York City, June 19, 1990.

93. Michael Butler interview.

94. Alvin Klein, "1960s *Hair* in Bridgeport Revival," *The New York Times* (April 6, 1989): Sec. 12, 18.

95. "Revival of *Hair* Transfers in Florida," *Variety* (April 19, 1989): 16.

96. *Variety* (April 19, 1989), 16.

97. Alvin Klein, "The Age of Aquarius, 2 Decades Later," *The New York Times* (May 7, 1989): Sec. 12, 27.

98. Klein (May 7, 1989), 27.

99. Klein (May 7, 1989), 27.

100. Castelli interview.

101. Castelli interview.

Chapter 6

The Impact of *Hair*

When it comes to evaluating *Hair*'s impact upon the theater arts, most scholars place the piece on the shoals of the Broadway musical mainstream. Commercially, *Hair* was enormously successful, and its box office record did stimulate a spate of rock musicals, however short-lived. By 1975 or thereabout, the form had played itself out. Rather than ushering in a joyous wedding of rock and theater, Broadway failed to integrate the new sound. In dismissing *Hair* because of its antiestablishment music and/or its lack of plot, many critics at the time failed to recognize its significance. Although *Hair* appeared to be a unique departure from conventional theater and the integrated book form, it did have antecedents within both the American musical theater and the off-Broadway avant-garde. Using experimental techniques in an organic workshop approach to the Broadway production, O'Horgan allowed the staging of *Hair* to evolve, the collective ensemble making their contributions to the development of the piece.[1] In an emphasis on production visuals, O'Horgan, Ragni, and Rado liberated the musical form from its dramatic trappings, putting the theatrical back in theater. Thus, *Hair* became Broadway's first fully realized concept musical, a form that would come to dominate the theater of the seventies.

Hair brought experimental techniques and rock music to

Broadway. While critics acknowledged the piece as revolutionary in its nonbook approach, they failed to recognize the rock musical as a concept musical because (1) it was rock, and (2) it was not from the esthete Hal Prince.

Robbins and Prince had already blazed the trail for the concept musical with *West Side Story, Fiddler on the Roof*, and *Cabaret* (see Chapter 1). Prince is recognized as having fully developed the concept musical with *Company* (1970). This "plotless" George Furth-Stephen Sondheim musical was considered revolutionary in its assembly of group relationships into a cinematic script, a development pioneered in *Hair*. While Prince refined his highly artistic and intellectual approach with *Follies, A Little Night Music*, and *Pacific Overtures* (1976), his protegé Michael Bennett took the credit for popularizing the concept musical with *A Chorus Line* (1975): "no longer a special show for people with refined taste."[2] Again, *Hair* had set precedent.

Making comparisons, *A Chorus Line* was scripted entirely from the collaborative creativity generated during an extended experimental workshop period subsidized by the Public Theater. First performed as a workshop production at the Public on April 15, 1975, it was mounted as a full-scale musical at the Public's Newman Theatre on May 21 before being transferred to the Shubert Theatre on July 25. Created by establishment theater people, *A Chorus Line* encountered no particular problems finding a house; of course, Marvin Hamlisch's score was not rock. Unlike *Hair*, *A Chorus Line* received numerous Tony awards, but similarly its commercial success kept the Public Theater running for many years. The parallels between the two productions abound—the organic workshop approach, the ensemble, the collaborative input, no overture, no curtain, minimal set, everyday (rehearsal) costumes. While Bennett used experimental techniques, his chorus did not mingle freely with the audience as did the untethered flower children of *Hair*: the group of neurotic dance gypsies were made to "toe the line." And within three weeks Bennett was rehearsing three touring companies simultaneously—a business lesson learned from *Hair*.

Hair was the first fully realized concept musical on Broadway. It was the first to bring the concept musical to mass audiences. Somewhat after the fact, O'Horgan did receive recognition for his contribution to the form. In *Ten Seasons: New York Theatre in the Seventies*, theater historian Samuel Leiter ranks O'Horgan among the new breed of concept musical directors like Bob Fosse, Gower Champion, Harold Prince, and Michael Bennett who "found success such as had rarely crowned the work of their gifted but less theatrically dominating predecessors."[3] And even Martin Gottfried, who coined the term "concept musical," conceded, "Yes, *Hair* on Broadway was a concept musical."[4]

THE ROCK MUSICAL

In his opening night review Gottfried wrote of *Hair*, "It has nothing to do with the Broadway musicals, whose formula has been slavishly followed for so long that with only a few exceptions they remain old-time song-and-dance shows. Considering the pop music phenomenon now in progress, the uniqueness of *Hair* proves how backward Broadway really is."[5]

Hair on Broadway *was* unique. It was Broadway's first rock musical. While the show did not contain a single authentic rock song, elements of rock music permeated the score: the rock rhythms and back beats, and the electrical instrumentation, particularly the lead guitar, bass guitar, and keyboard, which constitute the core of a rock band. The new sound had appeared on Broadway before *Hair* in the 1950s musical *Bye-Bye Birdie* with its few popular, if "impure," rock numbers, and in *West Side Story* with its musical pieces with rock; but the Ragni and Rado piece was the first to use rock instrumentation throughout.

In its use of the vernacular, *Hair* appears to have influenced the instrumentation of subsequent shows. Papp presented an updated version of *Hamlet*, sometimes referred to as the "Naked" *Hamlet* (the second production after *Hair*), which featured rock music. In January 1968, the Shakespearean rock musical, *Your Own Thing*, based loosely upon *Twelfth Night*, opened at the off-Broadway Orpheum, the second American rock musical to attain national and international success. Throughout the early 1970s, both on and off Broadway, some musicals used rock numbers. In 1971, MacDermot composed the tunes for yet another rocked-up version of Shakespeare, a contemporary *Two Gentlemen of Verona*. Still other rock musicals that followed *Hair* combined rock pieces with semireligious themes, such as *Godspell* and *Jesus Christ Superstar*.

Stephen Schwartz's successful, small-scale, semi-rock musical *Godspell* began as librettist John Tebelak's master's degree thesis at Carnegie Tech, was first presented at LaMama, moved to the Cherry Lane, and finally to the Promenade uptown.

The more elaborate *Jesus Christ Superstar* also dealt with the last days of Christ. Creators Andrew Lloyd Webber and Tim Rice freely admit their decision to write a rock show came immediately after they attended a performance of *Hair* at the Biltmore.[6] Unable to get the show on the boards, they cut the album to promote it, and it was ultimately staged on Broadway in 1971. Directed by O'Horgan, the "rock opera," with no dialogue whatsoever, was a circus of gaudy spectacle and amplified sound. While the show offended many, including some religious sects, the producer maintained the musical was antiestablishment, not antireligion.

In 1972, the staging of Ragni and MacDermot's *Dude, or the Highway of Life* called for a complete revamping of the Broadway Theatre into a multifocus "terrain" that extended into portions of the orchestra. The intent was to "tear the theater apart,'' said Ragni. Patrons purchased tickets to sit in the ''valleys'' or the ''trees'' or, higher up, in the ''mountains.'' Midway through rehearsals *Dude*'s director was dismissed. O'Horgan was brought in to save the show. However, as MacDermot contended, *Dude* ''had some nice things in it,'' but the show wasn't saveable.''[7] Producers Peter and Adela Holzer lost close to a million dollars on the experimental fiasco, which closed after sixteen performances and signaled the beginning of the end to Broadway's infatuation with the rock and youth culture. (As an interesting aside, Hal Prince moved into the gutted Broadway Theatre to stage the highly acclaimed, environmental [revised] revival of Bernstein's *Candide*; Ragni's odyssey into the audience was upstaged by Voltaire's successful peregrinations, also into the audience.)

In 1972, Rado produced the off-Broadway *Rainbow*, which opened at the Orpheum. He wrote the music and lyrics for the anti-Vietnam War piece about a casualty who ascends in death to radio heaven. The show received favorable notices from the major critics, but closed in three weeks. Rado confided that he knew nothing about producing and promoting a show, or about getting audiences to the East Village of the time.

In 1972, Galt MacDermot wrote the score of *Via Galactica*, which opened the Uris Theatre (subsequently renamed the Gershwin). Under Peter Hall's direction, the show folded in a week. *Grease* (1972), which reverted to the rock sounds of the fifties, opened off-Broadway, soon being transferred to Broadway where it became a phenomenal success, second only to *A Chorus Line* in length of run on Broadway.

In 1974, O'Horgan staged *Sgt. Pepper's Lonely Hearts Club Band on the Road* with its thin plot and the usual pyrotechnics at the Beacon Theatre. The show ran for eight weeks. The all-black musical *The Wiz* (1975), a mixture of rock, gospel, and soul music, was a smash hit. In 1976,

Rockabye Hamlet opened at the Minskoff. Under Gower Champion's direction, the creators attempted unsuccessfully to repeat the Shakespearean rock equation with songs like "The Rosencrantz and Guildenstern Boogie."

Despite the initial upstart, the rock musical did not evolve into a significant subgenre. In O'Horgan's estimation, there were other rock musicals that came after *Hair*, but they were "lopped off by the establishment thereby destroying any nurturing process."[8]

Responding to the statement that there were a few rock musicals, Barnes said that rock had little or no influence: "There really weren't any rock musicals. No major rock musician ever did a rock score for Broadway. There's a possibility that the Kinks are doing one at the moment. You might think of the musical *Tommy*, but it was never conceived as a Broadway show. *Jesus Christ Superstar* had some elements of rock, but not many. Lloyd [Andrew Lloyd Webber] is hardly a rock composer."[9] Lennon and McCartney were rock composers. The Beatles could have easily written a musical, but they didn't. "And one can see why," Barnes speculated. "There's so much more money in records and rock concerts. I mean, why bother going through the pain of a musical which may close in Philadelphia?"[10]

Critics had hoped for a synthesis of musical comedy and rock, but aside from *Your Own Thing, Godspell, Jesus Christ Superstar*, and one or two others, no such synthesis took place. Such failures may have been the result of producers simply relying on the label "rock musical" to attract audiences without regard to the quality of the material presented, or they may not have been able to compete with alternative types of rock theater, such as rock concerts, or perhaps pure rhythm music is simply unsuited for the needs of integrated musicals. Whatever the reasons, it does seem clear that rock composers opted for the more lucrative outlet of rock concerts, and that *Hair* did not bring on a lasting "'rock musical'" subgenre.

NEW AUDIENCES

Rock spoke the language of youth, and as a rock musical, *Hair* opened up a terrific new audience for the theater. "I'm not a rock musician," said O'Horgan. "Basically, I'm not interested in rock. I don't think that rock has had one new idea in the last twenty years, but at that particular time, it was the vital form of music. The best composers were composing it, and it brought new audiences to Broadway."[11]

In the *Hair* Biltmore Souvenir Program O'Horgan stated his intention to attract new people to Broadway by a fresh, venturesome theater that had immediacy: "We hope—and think—that *Hair* will reach out to create a whole new audience for the Broadway theatre. I would say the theatre's greatest hope for coming alive again and being fully relevant to us all, is to produce the kind of work that would interest people in college today. If we don't, we might as well tear the remaining theaters down and pave them for parking lots."[12]

The dream was realized. As the show's reputation grew, so did the proportion of young people in the audience. The audiences at the Public Theater tended to be conventional middle-class theatergoers, as was the directorial vision. The Cheetah audiences were younger, but whether they were attracted to the discotheque because of *Hair* or because they were regular Cheetah patrons cannot be determined. At the Biltmore, there appeared to be a departure from the general demographics of Broadway theatergoers. A little more than four months after opening night at the Biltmore, *New York* magazine's George Nash conducted an informal sampling of *Hair*'s patrons. Forty-six percent were under thirty, only 13 percent were fifty or over, and 7 percent were black, all of them under thirty.[13]

The trend toward youthful audiences continued. Following the Nash survey, the *Wall Street Journal* reported the outcome of a similar head count taken in June 1969. The *Journal*'s tally revealed that one half of *Hair*'s audience was between the ages of eighteen and twenty-five, as compared to 3 percent for other Broadway productions.[14] Thus, the show had been unmistakably successful in turning on a younger generation of theatergoers to Broadway for the first time.

Hair opened the doors for black actors and black audiences. The message was not black. As tribe member Lorrie Davis says, "Blacks couldn't afford to be hippies."[15] The show related more to white suburban youth and their problems, but it was the black kids who carried the show. *Hair* was the first racially integrated musical; one third of the cast was black. An *Ebony* magazine article proclaimed that the musical was the biggest outlet for black actors in the history of the U.S. stage.[16]

With a cast that was one third black, the show succeeded in bringing black audiences to the theater for the first time. George Tipton, a black member of the Biltmore tribe, commented that the few blacks who saw the show were proud of the contributions of their performers on Broadway.[17] If *Hair* didn't speak directly to black audiences, it did use black talent; it did address civil rights issues; and it did play a major role in the emergence of black performers, black playgoers, black creators, and black musicals on Broadway.

FIRST AMENDMENT RIGHTS

Hair struck many blows for freedom, for individual freedom, for First Amendment rights. The first Broadway musical to display complete nudity of both males and females, *Hair* turned *Marat/Sade*'s naked actor around and gave the Scarsdale ladies a glimpse of the male member.[18] It broke the barriers restraining nudity and profanity on the Broadway stage. *Hair*'s nudity helped to define permissible limits of free expression within the American theater when the United States Supreme Court twice issued major decisions concerning First Amendment rights based on the show (Boston and

Chattanooga). The Ragni and Rado piece was a forerunner to later pieces such as *Oh! Calcutta!* that provided the audience with prolonged and well-lit view of naked male and female actors in motion. Although the nudity and obscenity of *Hair* may seem tame by today's standards, the show was extremely controversial in its time.

THE IMPORTANCE OF *HAIR*

Hair was the first Broadway musical devoted to the hippie counterculture of the late 1960s. It was very much a kind of poster of the sixties, an agit-prop musical. As Clive Barnes of the *New York Times* wrote to his readers, it is "so likable, so new, so fresh and so unassuming, even in its pretensions. It is the first Broadway musical in some time to have the authentic voice of today rather than the day before yesterday."[19] The musical is a reflection of the emotional turmoil of the Vietnam War years with its concomitant antiestablishment, peace-love movement that produced a generation of drug-oriented, sexually liberated, social dropouts. The musical is a study of the lifestyles of the hippies and flower children who welcomed the dawning of the Age of Aquarius by opposing the draft, the work ethic, and accepted standards of behavior and dress.

Joseph Papp's selection of the musical as the show to open the Public Theater was based primarily on his perception of its social relevance. As an exposure of a counterculture, the musical was both a depiction of the hippie lifestyle and a critique of the parent culture against which the hippies defined themselves. The show included protests against the attitudes of the parent culture on such issues as war and racial inequality while commenting on alternative issues as well.

The outward manifestations of the hippie lifestyle were recreated in the show through costuming, communal rituals (especially those involving psychedelic drugs), and beginning with the Biltmore production, nudity. The show's dialogue and lyrics expressed the philosophical assumptions of the hippies, including their rejection of "scientific objectivity" and their complementary adoption of mysticism. A spiritual theme runs throughout the play; outer space, astrology, the earth, the heavens, interplanetary travel, mysticism, as noted in the songs "Aquarius," "Walking in Space," "Good Morning Starshine," and "Exanaplanetooch."

Loose structure, disregard for Aristotelian plot and rounded characterizations, use of hippie jargon and rock instrumentation, and a blurring of the line between art and life gave *Hair* a form expressive of the beliefs and practices of the hippies.

The "fourth wall" had been assaulted by Broadway musicals long before *Hair* opened at the Biltmore. As early as *Of Thee I Sing*, producers had used techniques to eliminate this perceived barrier. The Ragni and Rado piece, however, was more radical in its efforts to tear it down. While Broadway shows of the past had sought to dispel the illusion of the proscenium arch, *Hair* sought a direct extension from the theater to the streets ouside. The techniques used in *Hair* to break down the fourth wall represented both an attack on theatrical conventions and an effort to establish continuity between what was happening in the streets surrounding the theater.

Was *Hair* a sincere, authentic reflection of the hippie movement? Left-wing detractors argued that the musical did not accurately reflect the hippie counterculture, and negated *Hair*'s claims of being an extension of what was happening in the streets. Their strongest argument centered on what they referred to as commerical exploitation, monetary rewards being anathema to the movement.

The authors' original intent was to stage *Hair* on Broadway. As O'Horgan stated, the decision to bring *Hair* to Broadway was in part the result of the perceived need to expose an unorthodox worldview to audiences with traditional orientations. As such, the show was an attempt to interpret and make intelligible an exotic social movement rather than to reproduce it meticulously. In order to reach viewers who could benefit most from exposure to an alternative lifestyle, the show departed from "realistic" presentation, functioning as an interpretation for those unfamiliar with the youth culture. And audiences, who considered St. Mark's Place off limits, did venture to the Biltmore to safely witness the cultural curiosities.

As the hippies were an eclectic group, the causes of the movement quite diverse, no consensus is available about what constituted an authentic hippie. Therefore, it seems perfectly understandable that some "hip" critics considered the show's claims of representation fraudulent simply because they occupied a different position within the broad spectrum of hippiedom. But in the final analysis, *Hair* is a piece of dramatic art. The matter of whether its participants actually believed in the countercultural principles espoused onstage seems of little or no importance.

As to its legacy, *Hair* revolutionized theater and the way of thinking, about not only theater, but about a way of life, an attitude, a philosophy. As LaMama's Ellen Stewart commented:

> The Beatles came, very straight up, hair a little long, three-piece suits, shirts, and ties. This was their scene. But *Hair* came with blue jeans, comfortable clothing, colors, beautiful colors, sounds, movement. . . . And you can go to AT&T, and see a secretary today, and she's got on blue jeans. . . .[20]
>
> You can go to the Philippines, you can go to Indonesia, you can go to Russia, you can go to Rumania, you can go to France, to Germany, to Italy, to Africa, you can go to Australia, you can go anywhere you want, and what *Hair* did, it is still doing *twenty years later*, and this came from Tom O'Horgan. A kind of emancipation, a spiritual emancipation that came from his staging. Now his staging was based on the vision of these two boys [Ragni and Rado], so it was not his alone, but he took the vision and made it possible for the world to share. . . .[21]
>
> And I'm saying that *Hair* until this date has influenced

every single thing that you see on Broadway, off-Broadway, off-off-Broadway, anywhere in the world, you will still see elements of the experimental techniques that *Hair* brought not just to Broadway, but to the entire world.[22]

As the sixties have had a dramatic effect upon the basic values of our culture, *Hair* has had an enduring impact on theater. And what *Hair* and the sixties continue to represent is the promise of American life in the future—because many of the questions they addressed still have not been answered.

NOTES

1. Interview with Tom O'Horgan, New York City, March 13, 1991.

2. Martin Gottfried, *Broadway Musicals* (New York: Harry N. Abrams, 1979), 37.

3. Samuel Leiter, *Ten Seasons: New York Theatre in the Seventies* (Westport, Conn.: Greenwood Press, 1986), 102.

4. Interview with Martin Gottfried, New York City, April 19, 1990.

5. Martin Gottfried, *Opening Nights: Theater Criticism of the Sixties* (New York: G. P. Putnam, 1969), 103-105.

6. Gottfried interview.

7. Interview with Galt MacDermot, New York City, June 29, 1990.

8. Interview with Tom O'Horgan, New York City, April 13, 1990.

9. Interview with Clive Barnes, New York City, April 19, 1990.

10. Barnes interview.

11. O'Horgan interview, 1990.

12. O'Horgan, *Hair*, Biltmore Souvenir Program.

13. George Nash, "What People Think of *Hair*," *New York Magazine* (September 6, 1968): 60.

14. "Shaggy Show Story," *The Wall Street Journal* (June 11, 1969). Clippings, Theatre Collection, New York Public Library.

15. Interviews with Lorrie Davis, April 26, 1990, and May 18, 1990.

16. Helen H. King, "*Hair*: Controversial Musical Is Biggest Outlet for Black Actors in U.S. Stage History," *Ebony* (May 1970): 120-121.

17. King, 120-121.

18. Goldman, p. 385.

19. Clive Barnes, "Theatre: *Hair*—It's Fresh and Frank; Likable Rock Musical Moves to Broadway," *The New York Times* (April 30, 1968). Clippings, Theatre Collection, New York Public Library.

20. Interview with Ellen Stewart, New York City, May 15, 1990.

21. Stewart interview.

22. Stewart interview.

Appendix A

Staff and Cast for *Hair* at the Public Theater, December 2, 1967

Staff

Producer	Joseph Papp
Associate Producer	Bernard Gersten
Book & Lyrics	Gerome Ragni and James Rado
Music	Galt MacDermot
Director	Gerald Freedman
Musical Director	John Morris
Scenery	Ming Cho Lee
Costumes	Theoni V. Aldredge
Lighting	Martin Aronstein
Band	Greg Ferrara
	Steve Gillette
	Jimmy Lewis
	Galt MacDermot
	Leonard Seeds

Cast

Dione	Jonelle Allen
"Dad"	Ed Crowley
Claude	Walker Daniels
Woof	Steve Dean
Jeannie	Sally Eaton

"Mom"	Marijane Maricle
Sheila	Jill O'Hara
Crissy	Shelley Plimpton
Berger	Gerome Ragni
Hud	Arnold Wilkerson
Susan	Susan Batson
Linda	Linda Compton
Suzannah	Suzannah Norstrand
Alma	Alma Robinson
Charlie	Warren Burton
Thommie	Thommie Bush
Bill	William Herter
Paul	Paul Jabara
Bob	Bob Johnson
Jim	Edward Murphy, Jr.

Staff and Cast for *Hair* at the Biltmore Theatre, April 29, 1968

Staff

Producer	Michael Butler
Executive Producer	Bertrand Castelli
Book & Lyrics	Gerome Ragni and James Rado
Music	Galt MacDermot
Director	Tom O'Horgan
Musical Director	Galt MacDermot
Dance Director	Julie Arenal
Scenery	Robin Wagner
Costumes	Nancy Potts
Lighting	Jules Fisher
Sound	Robert Kiernan
Band	Warren Chaisson
	Alan Fontaine
	Donald Leight
	Jimmy Lewis
	Galt MacDermot
	Leo Morris
	Neil Tate
	Eddy Williams
	Zane Paul Zacharoff

Cast

Claude	James Rado
Ron	Ronald Dyson
Berger	Gerome Ragni
Woof	Steve Curry
Hud	Lamont Washington
Mother	Sally Eaton
	Jonathan Kramer
	Paul Japara
Father	Robert I. Rubinsky
	Suzannah Norstrand
	Lamont Washington
Jeanie	Sally Eaton
Dionne	Melba Moore
Sheila	Lynn Kellogg
Tourist Couple	Shelley Plimpton
	Jonathan Kramer
	Robert I. Rubinsky
Crissy	Shelley Plimpton
General Grant	Paul Jabara
Young Recruit	Jonathan Kramer
Parents	Diane Keaton
	Robert I. Rubinsky
The Tribe	Donnie Burks
	Lorrie Davis
	Leata Galloway
	Steve Gamet
	Walter Harris
	Diane Keaton
	Hiram Keller
	Marjorie LiPari
	Emmaretta Marks
	Natalie Mosco
	Suzannah Norstrand
	Robert I. Rubinsky

Appendix C

Staff and Cast for *Hair* Revival at the Biltmore Theatre, October 5, 1977

Staff

Producer	Michael Butler in association with K. H. Nezhad
Associate Producer	George Milman
Book & Lyrics	Gerome Ragni and James Rado
Music	Galt MacDermot
Director	Tom O'Horgan
Choreography	Julie Arenal
Assistant Choreographer	Wesley Fata
Scenery	Robin Wagner
Costumes	Nancy Potts
Lighting	Jules Fisher
Sound	Denzil A. Miller
Production Stage Manager	J. Galen McKinley
Band	Muhammad Abdullah
	Chris Alpert
	Danny Bank
	Billy Butler
	Rick Cutler
	Richard Hurwitz
	Jerry Jemmott
	Brian Koonin
	Denzil A. Miller

Vocal Director   Patrick Flynn

Cast (in order of appearance)

Claude   Randall Easterbrook
Berger   Michael Hoit
Woof   Scott Thornton
Hud   Cleavant Derricks
Sheila   Ellen Foley
Jeanie   Iris Rosenkrantz
Dionne   Alaina Reed
Crissy   Kristern Vigard
Shopping Cart Lady   Michael Leslie
Mothers   Annie Golden
                                  Louis Mattioli
                                  Perry Arthur
Fathers   James Rich
                                  Eva Charney
                                  Martha Wingate
Principals   Carl Woerner
                                  Michael Leslie
                                  Linda Myers
Tourist Couple   Perry Arthur
                                  Carl Woerner
General Grant   Carl Woerner
Abraham Lincoln   Linda Myers
Sergeant   Brian Utley
Parents   Lorie Wagner
                                  James Rich
Tribe   Perry Arthur
                                  Emily Bindiger
                                  Paul Binotto
                                  Eva Charney
                                  Loretta Devine
                                  Peter Gallagher

Doug Katsaros

Michael Leslie

Louis Mattioli

Linda Myers

Raymond Patterson

James Rich

James Sbano

Deborah Van Valkenburgh

Lori Wagner

Doug Wall

Martha Wingate

Carl Woerner

Charlaine Woodard

Appendix D

Staff and Cast for the Motion Picture Version of *Hair*, 1979

Staff

Producers	Lester Persky
	Michael Butler
Associate Producer	Richard Greenhut
Director	Milos Forman
Assistant Director	Michael Hausman
Screenplay	Michael Weller
Lyrics	Gerome Ragni and James Rado
Music	Galt MacDermot
Photography	Miroslav Ondricek
Choreography	Twyla Tharp
Designer	Stuart Wurtzel
Costumes	Ann Roth
Editor	Lynzee Kingman

Cast

Claude	John Savage
Berger	Treat Williams
Sheila	Beverly D'Angelo
Jeanie	Annie Golden
Hud	Dorsey Wright
Woof	Don Dacus

Hud's Fiancée	Cheryl Barnes
Fenton	Richard Bright
The General	Nicholas Ray
Party Guest	Charlotte Rae
Steve	Miles Chapin
Sheila's Mother	Fern Tailer
Sheila's Father	Charles Deney
Sheila's Uncle	Herman Meckler
Sheila's Aunt	Agnes Breen
Berger's Mother	Antonia Rey
Berger's Father	George Manos
Vietnamese Girl	Linda Surh
Debutantes	Jane Booke
	Suki Love
Claude's Father	Joe Acord
Sheldon	Michael Jeter
Prison Psychiatrist	Janet York
Lafayette Jr.	Rahsaan Curry
The Judge	Harry Gittleson
The MP	Donald Alsdurf
Barracks Officer	Mario Nelson

Bibliography

BOOKS AND COLLECTED ARTICLES

Belz, Carl. *The Story of Rock*. New York: Oxford University Press, 1972.

Berger, Peter, and Thomas Luckman. *The Social Construction of Reality*. Garden City, N.Y.: Doubleday Press, 1966.

Blau, Eric. *jacques brel is alive and well and living in paris*. New York: E. P. Dutton, 1971.

Bordman, Gerald. *American Musical Theatre: A Chronicle*. New York: Oxford University Press, 1978.

Brake, Mike. *The Sociology of Youth Culture and Youth Subcultures*. London: Routledge & Kegan Paul, 1980.

Brockett, Oscar G. and Robert R. Findlay. *Century of Innovation: A History of European and American Theatre since 1870*. Englewood Cliffs, N.J.: Prentice-Hall, 1973.

Cavan, Sherri. *Hippies of the Haight*. St. Louis: New Critics, 1972.

Chisnall, Arthur, Brian Lewis, and Auriel Hall. *Unattached Youth*. London: Blond and Briggs, 1974.

Cook, Bruce. *The Beat Generation*. New York: Charles Scribner, 1971.

Davis, Fred. *On Youth Subcultures: The Hippie Variant*. New York: General Learning Press, 1971.

Davis, Lorrie and Rachel Gallagher. *Letting Down My Hair*. New York: Arthur Fields, 1971.

Earisman, D. L. *Hippies in Our Midst*. Philadelphia: Fortress Press, 1968.

Engel, Lehman. *Words with Music*. New York: Macmillan Press. 1972.

Elson, John. *Erotic Theatre*. New York: Taplinger Press, 1973.

Ewen, David. *The New Complete Book of the American Musical Theater*. New York: Holt, Rinehart and Winston, 1970.

Gardner, Hugh. *The Children of Prosperity: Thirteen Modern American Communes*. New York: St. Martin's Press, 1978.

Garfinkel, Harold. *Studies in Ethnomethodology*. Englewood Cliffs, N.J.: Prentice-Hall, 1967.

Gassner, John. *Directions in Modern Theatre and Drama*. New York: Holt, Rinehart and Winston, 1967.

Goldman, William. *The Season: A Candid Look at Broadway*. New York: Harcourt, Brace & World, 1969.

Gottfried, Martin. *Opening Nights: Theater Criticism of the Sixties*. New York: G. P. Putnam, 1969.

_____. *Broadway Musicals*. New York: Harry N. Abrams, 1979.

Greenberger, Howard G. *The Off-Broadway Experience*. New York: Harcourt, Brace & World, 1969.

Hayman, Ronald. *Theatre and Anti-Theatre: New Movements since Beckett*. New York: Oxford University Press, 1979.

Hendin, Herbert. *The Age of Sensation*. New York: W. W. Norton, 1975.

Hostetler, John. *Communitarian Societies*. New York: Holt, Rinehart and Winston, 1974.

Hoffman, Abbie. *Revolution for the Hell of It*. New York: Dial Press, 1968.

Kenniston, Kenneth. *Young Radicals: Notes on Committed Youth*. New York: Harcourt Brace Jovanovich, 1968.

_____. *Youth and Dissent: The Rise of a New Opposition*. New York: Harcourt Brace Jovanovich, 1971.

Kirby, Michael, ed. *The New Theatre*. New York: New York University Press, 1974.

Kophart, William M. *Extraordinary Groups: The Sociology of Unconventional Life Styles*. New York: St. Martin's Press, 1976.

Lahr, John. *Up against the Fourth Wall*. New York: Grove Press, 1970.

Laing, R. D. *The Divided Self: An Existential Study in Sanity and Madness.* Harmondsworth, England: Penguin Books, 1960.

Laufe, Abe. *Broadway's Greatest Musicals.* New York: Funk & Wagnalls, 1969.

Leiter, Samuel. *Ten Seasons: New York Theatre in the Seventies.* Westport, Conn.: Greenwood Press, 1986.

Little, Stuart W. *Off-Broadway: The Prophetic Theater.* Englewood Cliffs, N.J.: Prentice-Hall, 1971.

Loney, Glen. "Musical Comedy." In *The Reader's Encyclopedia of World Drama.* Edited by John Gassner and Edward Quinn. New York: Thomas Y. Crowell, 1969, pp. 592-604.

Malcolm, Henry. *Generation of Narcissus.* Boston: Little, Brown, 1971.

Mandelkorn, Philip. "The Evolution of the Hippie." In *The Hippies.* Edited by Joseph David Brown. New York: Time, 1967.

_____. "The Flower Children." In *The Hippies.* Edited by Joseph David Brown. New York: Time, 1967.

Melville, Keith. *Communes in the Counter Culture.* New York: William Morrow, 1972.

Milson, Fred. *Youth in a Changing Society.* London: Routledge & Kegan Paul, 1972.

Mordenn, Ethan. *Better Foot Forward: The History of the American Musical Theatre.* New York: Grossman Press, 1976.

Partridge, William L. *The Hippie Ghetto: The Natural History of a Subculture.* New York: Holt, Rinehart & Winston, 1973.

Pasolli, Robert. *A Book on the Open Theatre.* Indianapolis: Bobbs-Merrill, 1970.

Perry, Charles. "The Gathering of the Tribes." In *The Sixties.* Edited by Joseph David Brown. New York: Random House, 1971.

Ragni, Gerome, and James Rado. "*Hair:* The American Tribal Love-Rock Musical." In *Great Rock Musicals.* Edited by Stanley Richards. New York: Stein and Day, 1979.

Revel, Jean François. *Without Marx or Jesus: The New American Revolution Has Begun.* New York: Dell Press, 1970.

Richards, Stanley, ed. *Great Rock Musicals* (New York: Stern and Day, 1979).

Roose-Evans, James. *Experimental Theatre: From Stanislavsky to Today*. New York: Avon Books, 1970.

Roszak, Theodore. *The Making of a Counter Culture*. Garden City, N.Y.: Doubleday, 1968.

Schwartz, Gary. *Beyond Conformity and Rebellion: Youth and Authority in America*. Chicago: University of Chicago Press, 1987.

Simon, John. *Uneasy Stages: A Chronicle of the New York Theatre, 1963–1973*. New York: Random House, 1975.

Strait, Guy. "What Is a Hippie?" In *Notes from the New Underground: An Anthology*. Edited by Jesse Kornbluth. New York: Viking Press, 1968, pp. 201-203.

Unger, Craig. *Blue Blood: How Rebekah Harkness, One of the Richest Women in the World, Destroyed a Great American Family*. New York: William Morrow, 1988.

Vulliamy, Graham. "Music and the Mass Culture Debate." In *Whose Music?: A Sociology of Musical Languages*. Edited by Howard S. Becker. New Brunswick, N.J.: Transaction Press, 1977.

Westhues, Kenneth. *Society's Shadows: Studies in the Sociology of Countercultures*. Toronto: McGraw-Hill/Ryerson, 1972.

Willis, John. *Theatre World: 1977-1978 Season*. New York: Crown, 1979.

Wilson, Edwin. *The Theatre Experience*, 4th ed. New York: McGraw-Hill, 1988.

Wilson, Garff B. *Three Hundred Years of American Drama and Theatre: From 'Ye Bear and Ye Cubb' to 'Hair'*. Englewood Cliffs, N.J.: Prentice-Hall, 1973.

Yablonski, Lewis. *The Hippie Trip*. New York: Pegasus Books, 1968.

PERIODICAL ARTICLES (SIGNED)

Auster, Al. "*Hair*." *Cineaste* (Spring 1979): 55-56.

Barnes, Clive. "*Hair*." *Saturday Evening Post* (September 8, 1977): 23.

Borzinger, John. "Whang! The Rock Musical." *Life* (December 26, 1969).

Brustein, Robert. "From *Hair* to *Hamlet.*" *New Republic* (November 18, 1967): 38-39.

Buchen, Irving H. "Is the Future *Hair.*" *Journal of Popular Culture* 3, no. 2 (Fall 1969): 324-332.

Clurman, Harold. "Clown and Hero." *New York* (May 20, 1968): 54.

Coldstream, John. "Theatre of Rock." *Plays and Players* 24, no. 6 (March 1977): 20-25.

Cowser, R. L. "Broadway Retrogresses: The Bookless Musical." *Journal of Popular Culture* 12, no. 3 (Winter 1978): 545-549.

Denby, David. "*Hair* Transplanted." *New York* (March 19, 1979): 62-63.

Deer, Harriet and Irving Deer. "Musical Comedy: From Performer to Performance." *Journal of Popular Culture* 12, no. 3 (Winter 1978): 406-421.

Dowling, Colette. "How *Hair* Found Fame and Fortune." *Playbill* (September 1968): 6-8.

_____. "*Hair:* Trusting the Kids and the Stars." *Playbill* (May 1971): 30-37.

Gilliatt, Penelope. "The Current Cinema: Fuzz." *New Yorker* (April 16, 1979): 142-143.

Gold, Ronald. "It's 'Non-Choreography,' But All Dance." *Dance Magazine* (July 1968): 29-30.

Harmon, James E. "The New Music and Countercultural Values." *Youth and Society* no. 4 (1972): 61-83.

Hewes, Henry. "The Theatre of Shattered Focus." *Saturday Review* (January 13, 1968): 95.

_____. "Blow-Ups." *Saturday Review* (May 11, 1968): 26.

Holland, Cecilia. "I Don't Trust Anybody under 30." *Saturday Evening Post* (August 10, 1968): 11.

Hornby, Richard. "The Decline of the American Musical Comedy." *The Hudson Review* 41, no. 1 (Spring 1988): 182-187.

Huffman, James R. "*Jesus Christ Superstar*—Popular Art and Unpopular Criticism." *Journal of Popular Culture* 6, no. 2 (Fall 1972): 259-270.

Kaiser, Charles. "A Roach Clip with Every Paid Subscription." *New York Times Book Review* (June 17, 1990): 7.

Kalem, T. E. "Theatre." *Time* (December 24, 1979): 77.

Kauffman, Stanley. "Ex-Champions." *The New Republic* (April 14, 1979): 40-41.

King, Helen H. "*Hair:* Controversial Musical Is Biggest Outlet for Black Actors in U.S. Stage History." *Ebony* (May 1970): 120-121.

Kolodin, Irving. "Music Returns to the Musical." *Saturday Review* (April 3, 1976): 43.

Kotlowitz, Robert. "*Hair:* Side, Back and Front Views." *Harper's Magazine* (September 1968): 107-109.

Lees, Gene. "*Hair* in Europe." *Hi Fidelity* (June 1970): 108.

Lewis, Theophilius. "*Hair.*" *America* (June 8, 1968): 759-760.

McCarthy, Todd. "Milos Forman Lets Down His *Hair.*" *Film Comment* (March-April 1979): 17-22.

Nash, George. "What People Think of *Hair.*" *New York* (September 6, 1968): 60-61.

Novick, Julius. "In Search of a New Consensus." *Saturday Review* (April 3, 1976): 39-42.

Prideaux, Tom. "*Hair:* That Play Is Sprouting Everywhere." *Life* (April 17, 1970): 63.

Richardson, Jack. "Avant-Garde Theatrics." *Commentary* (November 1968): 24.

Rockwell, John. "Long Hair?" *Opera News* (December 20, 1969): 9-13.

Weales, Gerald. "I Left It at the Astor." *Reporter* (April 1968): 36-39.

Westbrook, Colin L. "*Hair* Today," *Commonwealth* (May 25, 1979): 305-306.

Yinger, Milton. "Counterculture and Subculture." *American Sociological Review* (1960): 625-635.

PERIODICAL ARTICLES (UNSIGNED)

"Director of the Year." *Newsweek* (June 3, 1968): 102.

"*Hair* around the World." *Newsweek* (July 7, 1969). Clippings, Theatre Collection, New York Public Library.

"Optional Nudity in *Hair.*" *Esquire* (September 1968): 131.

"Supreme Court Letting the Sun Shine In." *Newsweek* (March 31, 1975): 37.

"Theater goes Public: New York Shakespeare Festival." *Players* (December 1969-January 1970): 56-61.

NEWSPAPER ARTICLES (SIGNED)

Aronowitz, Alfred G. *"Hair*'s Happy Birthday." *New York Post* (April 27, 1970): 2.

Barnes, Clive. Theater: *Hair*—It's Fresh and Frank; "Likable Rock Musical Moves to Broadway." *The New York Times* (April 30, 1968.) Clippings, Theatre Collection, New York Public Library.

_____. *"Hair* Holds Up under 2d Look." *The New York Times* (February 5, 1969): 36.

_____. "New *Hair.*" *The New York Times* (September 13, 1969): 30.

_____. "Untitled." *The New York Times* (January 13, 1970): C26.

_____. "Contemporary Youth Depicted in Play." *New York Post* (April 27, 1970): 2.

Beaufort, John. "Controversial *Hair.*" *The Christian Science Monitor* (March 15, 1970). Clippings, Theatre Collection, New York Public Library.

Bender, Marilyn. "Topless, and No Bottoms Either." *The New York Times* (April 28, 1968): D3.

Berkvist, Robert. "Melba Changes Color of *Hair.*" *The New York Times* (September 14, 1969). Clippings, Theatre Collection, New York Public Library.

Curtiss, Thomas Quinn. "Translated *Hair* Cheered in Paris." *The New York Times* (June 2, 1969). Clippings, Theatre Collection, New York Public Library.

D'Arcy, Kevin. "A Little Nudity Sells a Lot of Tickets." *London Sunday Telegraph* (September 20, 1969). Clippings, Theatre Collection, New York Public Library.

Eder, Richard. "Stage Revised *Hair* Shows Its Gray." *The New York Times* (October 1977), C22.

Ghisays, Robert. "Rome Test: Bracing for *Hair.*" *The Newark Evening News* (August 20, 1970): 46.

Glover, William. *"Hair* Is a Continuous Happening." *Newark Sunday News* (August 2, 1970): E4.

Green, Abel. "L'Affair *Hair* and the Astronauts Who Walked Out." *Variety* (June 18, 1970): 65.

Gussow, Mel. "Fair (Osaka) and *Hair* (Tokyo) Keep Producer

Busy." *The New York Times* (October 9, 1968). Clippings, Theatre Collection, New York Public Library.

Harris, William. "*Hair* Transplant." *Soho Weekly News* (September 8, 1977): 25-26.

———. "Theatre: A Man for All Seasons." *East-Side Express* (October 27, 1977): 9.

Hess, John L. "Salvation Army Jousts with *Hair* in Paris." *The New York Times* (February 2, 1970). Clippings, Theatre Collection, New York Public Library.

Hummler, Richard. "Untitled." *Variety* (October 30, 1967). Clippings, Theatre Collection, New York Public Library.

Jewell, Derek. "Still a Winner." *London Sunday Times* (June 30, 1974). Clippings, Theatre Collection, New York Public Library.

Kerr, Walter. "*Hair*: Not in Fear, but in Delight." *The New York Times* (May 19, 1968): D3.

Klein, Alvin. "1960s *Hair* in Bridgeport Revival." *The New York Times* (April 6, 1989): Sec. 12, 18-19.

———. "The Age of Aquarius, 2 Decades Later." *The New York Times* (May 7, 1989): Sec. 12, 26-27.

Kloman, William. "2001 and *Hair*—Are They the Groove of the Future?" *The New York Times* (May 12, 1968): D8.

Lewis, Anthony. "Londoners Cool to *Hair*'s Nudity." *The New York Times* (September 29, 1968). Clippings, Theatre Collection, New York Public Library.

Marriott, R. B. "The Freedom That Is *Hair*." *The Stage and Television Today* (October 31, 1968). Clippings Theatre Collection, New York Public Library.

Marcus, Frank. "A Splash of *Hair* Tonic." *London Sunday Telegraph* (September 29, 1968): 14.

———. "Graying *Hair*." *London Sunday Telegraph* (June 30, 1974). Clippings, Theatre Collection, New York Public Library.

Oppenheimer, Geroge. "On Stage." *The Newark Evening News* (June 8, 1968). Clippings, Theatre Collection, New York Public Library.

Otten, Alan T. "People Patterns." *The Wall Street Journal* (February 20, 1990): B1.

Palmer, Robert. "Writing Musicals Attuned to the Rock Era." *The New York Times* (February 10, 1982): C21.

Sandrow, Nahma. "What Will *Hair* Say to the 70s?" *The New York Times* (October 2, 1977): D26.

Schjeldahl, Peter. "Can *Hair* Be Taught to Hate?" *The New York Times* (September 27, 1970): 11.

Sullivan, Dan. "Papp Is a Love Person." *The New York Times* (October 15, 1967). Clippings, Theatre Collection, New York Public Library.

Taubman, Howard. "Untitled." *The New York Times* (November 13, 1967). Clippings, Theatre Collection, New York Public Library.

Walker, John. "*Hair* Is Back: Middle-Aged Spread." *International Herald Tribune* (June 29, 1974). Clippings, Theatre Collection, New York Public Library.

Warren, William K. "Attorney for *Hair* Irks Judge with Comment on Scopes Trial." *Chattanooga Times* (April 5, 1973): 1.

Wilson, Edwin. "A Look at *Hair* Six Years After." *The Wall Street Journal* (September 20, 1974): 7.

————. "The Rare Birds of Broadway." *The Wall Street Journal* (August 18, 1978). Clippings, Theatre Collection, New York Public Library.

Wilson, John S. "Rock Goes the Musical Theatre." *The New York Times* (October 15, 1967). Clippings, Theatre Collection, New York Public Library.

NEWSPAPER ARTICLES (UNSIGNED)

"Assert Madrid *Hair* Was Pirate Version," *Variety* (August 19, 1970). Clippings, Theatre Collection, New York Public Library.

"Desecration of the Flag Irks Hub More than Nudity in *Hair*." *Variety* (February 25, 1970). Clippings, Theatre Collection, New York Public Library.

"Earth Day Isn't Getting Any Easier." *The New York Times* (April 22, 1990): 13.

"Exit the Censor." *The Christian Science Monitor* (October 5, 1968): 18.

"Mexican Actors Favor *Hair* Deportation." *The New York Times* (January 8, 1968), C35.

"Mexico Shuts *Hair* and Expels Its Cast after One Showing." *The New York Times* (January 6, 1969): C43.

"In Popular Class, Lessons Concern the Vietnam War." *The New York Times* (February 25, 1990): 43-44.

"Producer Sues N.Y. Theater League on *Hair* Exclusions as Tony Entry." *Variety* (March 20, 1968). Clippings, Theatre Collection, New York Public Library.

"Revival of *Hair* Transfers in Florida." *Variety* (April 19, 1989): 16.

"Rock and Roll Musical Moving to Cheetah." *The New York Times* (December 6, 1967). Clippings, Theatre Collection, New York Public Library.

"Shaggy Show Story." *The Wall Street Journal* (June 11, 1969). Clippings, Theatre Collection, New York Public Library.

"Supreme Court Clears *Hair* for Boston Run." *The New York Times* (May 23, 1970), C27.

"Uncut *Hair* Reopens in Boston, Saved by Supreme Court Ruling." *Variety* (May 27, 1970): 57.

"Untitled." *The New York Times* (June 7, 1969). Clippings, Theatre Collection, New York Public Library.

"Untitled." *The New York Times* (September 5, 1970). Clippings, Theatre Collection, New York Public Library.

"Untitled." *The New York Times* (July 5, 1972). Clippings, Theatre Collection, New York Public Library.

INTERVIEWS

All interviews were conducted by the author in New York City, either face-to-face or via telephone.

Barnes, Clive. April 19, 1990.
Blau, Isabelle. March 31, 1990.
Butler, Joseph Campbell. June 28, 1990.
Butler, Michael. April 3, 1990.
Castelli, Bertrand. March 6, 1990.
Davis, Lorrie. April 26, 1990, and May 18, 1990.
DiFazio, William. November 5, 1990.
Fisher, Jules. September 1, 1981.

Freedman, Gerald. October 27, 1977 and April 10, 1990.
Gottfried, Martin. April 19, 1990.
MacDermot, Galt. August 11, 1980, and June 29, 1990.
Moore, Melba. June 19, 1990.
O'Horgan, Tom. November 4, 1977, March 9, 1982, and April 13, 1990.
Rado, James. March 3, 1990, March 11, 1990, and March 25, 1990.
Ragni, Gerome. March 3, 1990, March 11, 1990, and March 25, 1990.
Stewart, Ellen. May 15, 1990.
Wagner, Robin. June 19, 1981.

Index

About the Author

BARBARA LEE HORN is Assistant Professor in the Department of Speech, Communication Sciences, and Theatre at St. John's University. She has had production experience on Broadway, Off-Broadway, and in television. She is presently working on a study of the career of producer Joseph Papp.